Philip Allan
Publishers

A-Level

Exam
Success
Guide

Sociology
Essays

Julia Davitt

Titles available

A-Level

Sociology: Essays

Biology: Essays

British History, 1815–1951

Business Studies: Essays

Chemistry: Multiple Choice

Chemistry: Structured Questions
& Essays

Computing

Economics: Data Response

Economics: Essays

Economics: Multiple Choice

English: Practical Criticism

European History, 1789–1945

French

Geography: Essays

History: Europe of the Dictators,
1914–1945

Law: General Principles

Media Studies

Physics: Structured Questions &
Multiple Choice

Politics: Essays

Pure Mathematics

Religious Studies: The New Testament —
The Gospels

Religious Studies: The Philosophy
of Religion

Philip Allan Publishers Limited
Market Place
Deddington
Oxfordshire OX15 0SE

Telephone: 01869 338652

ISBN 0 86003 329 5

Typeset by Getset, Eynsham, Oxford and printed by Information Press, Eynsham, Oxford

Contents

Contents

Introduction

The purpose of this guide is to improve your examination grade. Many sociology students under-achieve, not because they don't know the content of the sociology syllabus, but because they cannot apply what they know to sociology questions. Rather than use the appropriate studies, some students use what examiners call the 'blunderbuss' approach – they write everything they know about a particular topic in the hope that some of the information will be right. This method does not tend to attract the highest grades; you should not hope that if you throw enough mud at a wall some of it will stick. In addition, many students have difficulty in evaluating the material that they know: they fail to provide supporting material and appropriate criticisms. Others achieve high sociology grades with little sociological knowledge purely because they have learnt application and evaluation skills. This guide aims to help you develop these skills. It covers the syllabuses of the Associated Examining Board and the Interboard and is suitable for both GCE A-level Sociology and GCE A/S-level Sociology.

I believe that there's a relationship between the way you prepare for the sociology exam and the grade you eventually achieve. You should use this volume as part of your exam preparation, and you should take the hints and tips it gives you and put them to work. The time to start this is now.

How to Use This Book

Each answer in this book provides a summary of some of the material for a given topic within sociology; thus the book is a useful revision aid. The contents are not model answers and it would not be wise to try and repeat them in examinations, or for homework, or for timed essays. To make the most of this book and improve your examination grade look at as many essays as possible, even if you are not studying those particular topics; for example, you may not be studying the topic of 'work and leisure' but you can still use the tips that I've given to help you with other topic areas. The reason for this is that each essay has different hints and tips which you will be able to apply to your own areas of study. In addition to tips on technique, you'll also be made aware of some of the mistakes which students frequently make in their answers. This will enable you to avoid these errors.

The Skills You Should Develop

The following skills are tested by the AEB and the Interboard syllabuses:

Knowledge and Understanding
You must know all the material for the topics which you intend to answer. Partial knowledge tends to result in a low grade; for example, suppose you revise 'education' but decide to leave out 'education and ethnicity', and when you come to sit the exam the question is on 'education and ethnicity'. This is 'Murphy's Law', if it can happen – it will happen. It does not matter how well you know 'gender and education', 'social class and education' and so on, you will not get a high grade if you do not know the relevant material. Examiners use a variety of terms to get you to show your knowledge and understanding, these include: 'Describe...', 'Examine the view...',

'Explain the view...', 'Give a definition of...', 'Name...', 'Outline...', 'List...', 'State...', 'What do sociologists mean by...?', 'What do you understand by...?', 'What is meant by...?'.

Interpretation and Application (sometimes called Analysis)

In the case of structured questions, in which you are given data in charts or graphs or written passages, you may have to pick out information such as trends, or do a simple calculation on percentages. As far as essays are concerned, the interpretation and application skills involve two easy tasks. Firstly, applying information from another area of the syllabus to the question. Secondly, applying examples from personal experience and/or from instances in contemporary society. In both these cases, the examples must be relevant. You will find lots of examples of these skills in this book and some tips on how to find your own examples. The following terms are used by the examiners to get you to show interpretation and application: 'According to Item A...', 'Examine...', 'Give an example of...', 'How might...?', 'Identify...', 'Illustrate with reference to...'.

Evaluation

Students tend to find this skill the most difficult and both the AEB and the Interboard give it higher marks. To evaluate sociological material does not mean ripping it apart like a hyperactive puppy with an old slipper. To evaluate successfully you must pick out the strengths and weaknesses of the theory or study which you have described. In simple terms, this means that you must identify what is good about the material and what is bad. In this book I've signposted the evaluations by the use of key words which signify evaluation. These terms include: 'however', 'on the other hand', or something as simple as 'an evaluation of Marx is found in the work of Weber who claimed that...'. These words serve two purposes. They tell the examiner that you are evaluating, and they encourage the examiner to award you marks for that evaluation. At some stage during your sociology course it's worth sitting down with other sociology students and brainstorming a list of words, terms and phrases which can be used to indicate evaluation. These words, terms and phrases also provide a good link to the next paragraph, so they can be used to structure your essays and make them flow.

Terms used by examiners to get you to show evaluation include: 'Assess', 'Consider the arguments for and against the view...', 'Discuss...', 'Evaluate...', 'Examine sociological contributions to...', 'Examine the evidence for and against...', 'How convincing...?', 'How far do...?', 'How successful...?', 'How useful is...?', 'Identify the strengths and weaknesses...', and finally 'To what extent...?'.

How to Revise Effectively

Start your revision now. First-year students may think that this advice about revision does not apply to them because they have all the time in the world. This is not the case. It's common for some students and lecturers/teachers to put a topic to bed once it has been completed and not look at it again until two weeks before the exam. Don't get caught out.

Revision involves work. Get yourself a syllabus, an empty lever-arch file, and copies of past exam papers from your examination board. Decide which areas of the syllabus you intend to cover in your exam. Most syllabuses have compulsory subjects: for the AEB it is 'theory and method', whereas for the Interboard it is 'stratification'. Make sure you know your compulsory subject. Find out how many topics you need to answer in total then choose the ones you prefer. Go through the past questions to discover what type of questions are likely to come up on your chosen topics; for example, in 'education' questions are likely to come up on the following areas – the role of education, the effects of recent education reforms, new vocationalism, education and social class, education and ethnicity, education and gender, the effects of schooling, the hidden curriculum. Once you have done this you will need to prepare the material (knowledge and understanding). You need to answer a question on every possible area within your chosen topics. Once you have your material ready for a specific area, abbreviate it so that it fits on one side of A4 paper, or even better, on a postcard. The names of researchers and the key points are enough; for example, from education 'Bernstein-Language'. When you are at this stage, turn over your paper or postcard and write it out from memory. Keep doing this until you get it right every time. At this point you will have the knowledge and understanding to apply to one question within one of your chosen topics. The next step is to take a question from your set of back copies of exam papers, and apply your knowledge to it using the tips on interpretation, application and evaluation which you've learned from this book. You should complete this task in the exact time which the examination allows for this question or part of a question. You should then get your tutor to check your efforts. This will enable you to make any necessary corrections to your notes. You must repeat this process until you have adequately covered each possible question within your chosen topics. At the end of this you will have filled the empty lever-arch file. You are now ready for the exam!

In the Exam Room

Read all the questions, then read all the questions again. Panic often leads to students misreading questions. Pick your favourite topic to do first, as this will give you confidence for the rest of the exam. It doesn't matter in what order you answer the questions. Show the examiner what you can do. They will be marking poor scripts all night and will be so pleased to see your excellent script. Some tutors advise against making essay plans in the exam room. I disagree with this. Providing your plans are brief, they often allow you to think about the structure of your answer as well as the content. However, you must do whatever works for you.

Finally, some writers and tutors will wish you luck – luck has nothing to do with examination success. All examination success depends on careful planning and preparation; nothing else will do the job as well. Therefore, I wish you good planning and good preparation.

Acknowledgements

I would like to thank Paul Davitt for his advice and support. I would also like to thank my children Hannah, Simon and Natalie for being patient and for making me endless cups of tea. Finally, I would like to thank my editor Richard Ball for his help and support.

Assess the strengths and weaknesses of interviews as a method of sociological enquiry.

Tackling the question

Essay titles which ask you to assess the strengths and weaknesses of a particular sociological method are a favourite of examiners. It means simply looking for what is good and what is bad about a particular approach or issue. The most important thing to do is offer a balance of strengths and weaknesses, in this case, of interviews. However, do be careful; if you concentrate on the strengths of interviews and just tag on the weaknesses, you will not be able to achieve high marks. You should also be aware that there are two types of interview, structured and unstructured. This means that you have to write about the strengths and weaknesses of both methods. There is a lot of information to cover in this essay and it is therefore essential that you plan your answer carefully. You will not do yourself any favours by mismanaging your time. You must aim for balance.

Answer

Guidance notes

There are two types of interview which tend to be used in sociological enquiry, structured interviews and unstructured interviews. Structured interviews involve the researcher working through a series of standardised questions. The wording of the question and the order in which the questions are given are predetermined, and are the same for all interviewees. By contrast, unstructured interviews involve the researcher having a list, schedule or *aide memoire* of topic areas which need to be discussed. The questions in this case are not predetermined. It is up to the researcher to phrase questions as s/he likes and to 'probe' particular responses.

Structured interviews are most commonly used in surveys, where they take the form of questionnaires, and are used to produce quantitative data. The questions in structured interviews are usually 'closed ended'. This means that a limited range of answers are provided for the interviewee to choose from. For example, did

In this introductory paragraph, I have identified the two different types of interview and their specific characteristics. This is always a good start because it acts as a springboard into the main body of the essay. You know from the introduction that a section of the essay will be given over to structured interviews, while another section will be given over to unstructured interviews. The introduction itself can act as a mini-essay plan.

The essay quickly moves on to the strengths of structured interviews. This is just like a

Question 1

'brainstorming' session with ifs, ands, and buts between the key words. This is an easy way to pick up marks for knowledge and understanding.

you vote in the last general election, yes or no? The major strength of using structured interviews as a method of sociological enquiry is that they are useful in providing a large amount of factual information in a short amount of time, at a relatively cheap cost. This method is most commonly used when the research involves large samples of respondents. A further strength is that the data collected are easily codified (translated into numerical form) and quantified (presented in numerical form, such as graphs). The data can be mathematically manipulated and this permits multi-variate analysis which allows the sociologist to look for cause and effect relationships.

An additional strength of using structured interviews is that the data obtained are considered reliable. This means that if the research were repeated at a later date, using the same methods and a similar research sample, then the results would be the same or similar to those of the first enquiry. This means that research which uses structured interviews is testable.

This paragraph introduces a critical analysis of structured interviews. Note how the essay is already showing balance. Again the criticisms are based on a memorised list of key words with ifs, ands, and buts between the words. Weaker students will spend a whole essay going over these basic points – fine if you are happy with a low grade.

Various criticisms have been made of structured interviews as a method of sociological enquiry. A serious weakness is that, while this method is useful when looking at straightforward factual information, it is less useful when trying to investigate more complex issues. The 'closed ended' nature of the questions means that the research cannot take up points of interest which may be uncovered throughout the research. The answer given by the interviewee is not open to further investigation. If the interviewee circles the response which indicates that s/he did not vote during the last election there is no way to find out why the individual acted in this way. Structured interviews therefore are weak in that they do not really provide the researcher with a means of achieving a true account of individuals' actions. There is no way to assess reasons and motives for behaviour and attitudes and no way to discover where such beliefs and attitudes come from. Thus, this method of sociological enquiry can be attacked for its lack of validity.

A further weakness of using structured interviews as a method of sociological enquiry is that the predetermined answers which are provided for the respondents may not truly represent the real opinions, views or beliefs of some of the sample. This could lead to respondents circling an answer which does not totally represent what they think or do. This could invalidate the research, in that the research may not be portraying a true account of the social area under investigation.

This paragraph switches the answer to the strengths of

An alternative method of sociological enquiry is the use of unstructured interviews. Unstructured interviews are usually used when more in-depth information is needed. They are usually used in research which involves a small sample of subjects, e.g. Oakley's study *The Sociology of Housework*, for which only 40 housewives were interviewed. Unstructured interviews are more likely to use 'open ended' questions which allow the interviewees to respond in any way they like. This method of enquiry also enables the researcher to follow up topics and issues of interest which may arise during the course of the interview.

The major strength of unstructured interviews is that they can produce qualitative information which looks further than statistics. Unstructured interviews can be used to uncover beliefs and motives for actions and attitudes. Those who use them believe that unstructured interviews provide information which is rich in validity, that is, that they produce a true picture of the social activity under investigation.

In addition, they are useful when studying areas which are not accessible to investigation by any other method. The research method of participant observation would have not been possible in Ann Oakley's investigation of housework.

Nevertheless, a number of criticisms have been put forward to show the weaknesses of unstructured interviews. Although they may be considered valid, they are not considered reliable. Each interview is individually tailored to each interviewee. This means that it is difficult to draw comparisons between different interviews. Consequently, it is difficult to generalise from the results of unstructured interviews to account for the actions, beliefs or attitudes of the population as a whole.

Interviews are always interactive situations. It can be argued that the status difference that sometimes exists between the interviewer and the interviewee may affect the responses of the respondent. The tone of voice, the types of clothing worn by the interviewer, the interviewer's accent and so on, may determine how the interviewee defines the situation and may govern the extent to which the interviewee 'opens up' in the interview process. Labov demonstrated both the interviewer-effect and the effect of surroundings in his study. He found that young black children responded differently to interview situations according to how they defined the situation. This demonstrates a serious weakness in unstructured interviews as a research method.

Labov's findings are supported in the work of Pierre who demonstrated that respondents sometimes give answers which they think the interviewer wants to hear, rather than their true opinions. In his 1930s study of racial discrimination in the United States, Pierre found discrepancies between what people said their attitudes were towards Chinese people and their behaviour.

unstructured interviews. Note the reference to Oakley. Try to use a relevant study to illustrate your point. You could get marks for application and evaluation if you do this. However, you only need one example per point, so don't get carried away.

You should note the words and phrases which are used to introduce each paragraph. Words such as: in addition, furthermore, moreover, are wonderful because they enable you to add more examples without them reading like a garbled list. Similarly, words such as: however, nevertheless, despite this, are equally as useful because they enable you to change direction in an essay from supporting to critical evidence. You might like to write a list of linking words or phrases which may prove useful for your general essay technique.

Now the essay has moved to criticising all types of interview. The example of self-report studies and youth crime is a good one to use as a critique because it covers two issues, the fact that people lie and the problem of basing a research method around memory. If you ever run out of things to criticise in any essay, try to introduce something about validity and reliability. This is guaranteed to earn you marks, providing of course that what you've said is relevant.

It can be argued that there are weaknesses in any type of interview as a method of sociological enquiry. One weakness is that the researcher has no way of knowing whether the interviewee is telling the truth or not. Interviewees may lie for a variety of reasons. If teenagers are given a 'self-report' survey to complete which asks them to list any crimes that they have committed, their answers may be determined by who is present at the time. If they complete the survey in front of a teacher or parent, they may 'forget' their criminal activities. On the other hand, if their friends are present, they may exaggerate their criminality in order to gain 'street credibility'. The researcher needs to be aware that what people *say* they do and what they *actually* do are not always the same thing. The idea that interviews can provide information which is rich in validity is open to criticism.

Another weakness in using interviews as a sociological research method is that people may not always be aware of what they do, and thus be unable to answer interview questions in these areas. This is demonstrated in the participant observation study carried out by Cicourel, called 'The Social Organisation of Juvenile Justice'. Cicourel found that police officers displayed taken-for-granted assumptions about juvenile offenders from different social-class backgrounds and labelled the offenders accordingly. He found that this labelling was an unconsidered part of the officers' daily activities and consequently could not have been revealed through the use of interviews.

The conclusion sums up the strengths and weaknesses of interviews as a method of sociological enquiry. You will note that I have ended the essay by suggesting an alternative approach to studying society. Don't be afraid to put your neck on the block, be brave and make a statement about which approach you believe to be best. However, don't forget to justify your choice.

In conclusion, although both structured and unstructured interviews have their weaknesses, they should not be discounted as methods of sociological enquiry. As a strength in one type of interview is often a weakness in the other, the two different types of interview can be used in one piece of research. This is known as methodological pluralism. This would give the researcher the opportunity to achieve both quantitative and qualitative data. Laud Humphreys demonstrates how interviews can be used in conjunction with participant observation in his study *Tearoom Trade* where he observed homosexual activity in public toilets. Humphreys attempted to interview some of the men he observed to clarify his observations. This, however, uncovered another problem with interviews: not everyone is prepared to be interviewed.

General Comments

You need a good knowledge and understanding of interviews to answer this question thoroughly. The advantages and disadvantages of different types of interviews can be used in other essays, and may be particularly useful when analysing a particular piece of research. For example, if you were writing an essay about housework, you could criticise Oakley's use of interviews as a research method. You would pick up points for evaluation by writing about some of the criticisms associated with the research method. You would also pick up marks for justifying why this approach was the best one to use. Some students will write essays about interviews as if there is only one type. This is to be avoided at all costs as it will prevent you from achieving the higher grades.

Related questions

1   Compare and contrast two methods of sociological enquiry.

2   Discuss the use of interviews in sociological research.

3   'Interview situations always contain an element of interaction, therefore they lack validity.' Evaluate this statement.

**Evaluate the uses and limitations
of participant observation as a method of
sociological enquiry.**

Tackling the question

This essay asks you to evaluate the uses and limitations of participant observation (PO). When you are asked to evaluate something, make sure you do just that. Aim to be as critical as possible because basic descriptions without critical analysis do not attract very high marks. In order to score highly for this particular essay, you must first offer support for the use of participant observation and then present a strong critique of participant observation as a method of sociological enquiry. Strong candidates should be able to offer justification of the method despite the criticisms. Use examples of investigations to demonstrate your points. Remember that you are being assessed on knowledge and understanding, application skills and your ability to evaluate.

Answer

In the first paragraph not only have I set the scene, but I have told the reader that I know the difference between positivist methodology and interactionist methodology.

Observation is used in every sociological study. For example, positivists may make observations by comparing various statistics, like Durkheim who compared the suicide rates of different countries and drew conclusions from the findings. However, interactionists argue against the methodology adopted by positivists. Interactionists believe that in order to investigate society, the researcher should make every effort to explore how social life is actually experienced by the individual, and examine the meanings which individuals put on their own behaviour. In order to do this, many interactionists use participant observation as their method of sociological enquiry.

The second paragraph offers a definition of PO and an explanation of the two different types of PO. Some students launch straight into examples of research which have used PO. I think it is

Participant observation involves 'participating', that is, joining in the activities of the group under investigation. However, the level of participation varies from researcher to researcher. Some researchers prefer to go undercover and not let their subjects know that they are being observed, while others prefer to be honest and ask their subjects' permission to be observed. The

former is k̲...̲ ...rvation, the latter as overt
particip...

...nt observation is the
...ining an insight into an
...orld and the only method
...r the actions of others. This
...icourel. Through participant
... find that police officers made
...al class which largely determined
... as a juvenile delinquent. Cicourel
...fficers were unaware that they were
...ased on labelling before they decided
to sto...̲ ...̲. If they had been given a questionnaire
or interviewe... ...ormation would not have been uncovered,
but participant ob...rvation *can* be used to uncover taken-for-
granted assumptions.

Participant observation is a method of sociological enquiry
which is considered to be rich in validity. This is because the
researcher is able to gain very detailed information which would
be difficult to elicit through any other method. This is shown in
Parker's work, *View from the Boys*. Parker claims that through
participant observation he was able to gain an understanding of
the behaviour displayed by a group of boys and the motivation
for their criminality. Parker argues that the insights which he
gained about the boys' criminal activities would probably not
have been uncovered using any other method of sociological
enquiry. While respondents may not give accurate responses to
questionnaires and interviews, the observer is in a position to ask
questions as and when they arise, and consequently can get a
truer account of social life as it is experienced by the individual.
The observer is able to find out what individuals actually do rather
than what they say they do. This is supported by Whyte, *Street
Corner Society*, who claims that his involvement in participant
observation gave him the opportunity to ask questions which he
would never have thought to ask in an interview situation.

In the case of questionnaires and interviews, the relationship
between the researcher and the subject is relatively short-lived.
A questionnaire may only take ten minutes to complete, then the
relationship between the researcher and the subject is over. In
comparison, participant observation is undertaken over a period
of time. This can be anything from several weeks to several years.
The nature of the relationship between the participant observer
and the observed may be much deeper, and a rapport and trust
usually develop. According to Yablonsky, *The Violent Gang*, when

important to set the scene and
acknowledge that there are two
types of PO.

You will notice that this paragraph
offers a brief description of the
uses of PO and provides an
example. Examples are good
because they demonstrate
application skills.

This paragraph, like the last,
demonstrates some advantages
of PO. Note how PO is used to
evaluate weaknesses in other
methodological approaches. It
may be a good idea to divide a
large piece of card into four
sections. Brainstorm all the
advantages of PO in one section,

and the disadvantages in another section. Then do the same for interviews. You could stick this up on your bedroom wall, not very cool I know, but according to my own students, it does work as a revision technique.

This paragraph introduces the limitations of PO. The reader knows that this is an evaluation because the paragraph starts with the word 'however'. This may seem simplistic, but it is effective. The use of key words like this is sometimes known as signposting.

This paragraph offers a counter criticism of participant observation. 'Nevertheless' is an excellent link word for this purpose. This is a good paragraph because it offers the three elements on which your performance is measured in the examination. It demonstrates knowledge and understanding, support for PO and a critique of PO – these are evaluations, and an applied study – which is an application skill.

members of the gang he was studying were issued questionnaires which aimed to investigate their personal activities, the gang looked at the questionnaire with distrust and suspicion. Participant observation is the best method of sociological enquiry to use when sensitive areas, such as gang culture, need to be investigated.

However, participant observation does have a number of limitations. Researchers may be limited in what they can study effectively. For example, it would have been difficult, if not impossible, for Oakley to use participant observation as a method of enquiry in her study of housework. In addition, researchers must take other factors into account when deciding to embark on a participant observation study, including their own sex, age and race. For example, a white female might find it difficult to become a participant observer of a black gang. Similarly, an older researcher might find it difficult to join a youth subculture.

Many researchers believe that research methods in sociology should be drawn from the natural sciences and are consequently critical of participant observation as a method of sociological enquiry. These researchers argue that a limitation of participant observation is that each study is unique to the particular group under investigation and therefore difficult to replicate. The data achieved via participant observation are not measurable. This means that there is no way of checking the reliability of the research, and that generalisations cannot be made from the results of the observational study to account for the actions of others. The observer cannot be sure that what was found through observation is representative of the whole population.

Nevertheless, those who support participant observation tend to argue that what participant observation lacks in reliability, it makes up in validity. However, the idea that participant observation leads to valid findings can also be questioned. There is a danger that the presence of an outsider can influence and change the behaviour of those being observed. This is known as the 'Hawthorne effect'. Whyte admitted that the researcher might influence the group under investigation. In the study *Street Corner Society*, the gang leader 'Doc' told Whyte that 'he slowed him down', so his presence had changed the behaviour of the group. Hence, Whyte's portrayal of the group under investigation may not have been a true picture.

Some researchers have attempted to control the 'Hawthorne effect' by becoming involved in covert participant observation rather than overt participant observation. However, even covert participant observation involves an outsider joining the group to be investigated, therefore natural behaviour cannot be guaranteed. In addition, there is a danger that the researcher may become over-involved in the activities of the group and may as a consequence be biased in the reporting of activities. This is known as 'going native'. There is no way of knowing if the researcher has retained objectivity in the course of the research.

Moreover, participant observation has practical limitations. Unlike questionnaires, conducting a participant-observation investigation is both time-consuming and expensive. The very nature of participant observation means that only one group can be investigated at a time. Research which uses participant observation as its method of enquiry may only be relevant to a particular time or place. It presents sociologists with a snap-shot of society rather than identifying laws which govern society.

In conclusion, although participant observation has some significant limitations, it also has a number of uses in sociology. It is difficult to imagine how an accurate study of gangs could be achieved without the use of participant observation as a method of sociological enquiry. In order to address the limitations of studies conducted by the use of participant observation, some researchers have adopted methodological pluralism, for example, Humphreys's *Tearoom Trade*, the observational study of male homosexual activity in public toilets, conducted follow-up interviews in order to test the validity of his original observations.

The concluding paragraph summarises the fact that PO has uses and limitations. You will note that the conclusion of the essay is similar to that of the previous essay. This is because the same information can on occasions be used in more than one essay as long as the information fits. In instances like this, there really is no need to reinvent the wheel.

General comments

Students tend to like participant observation as a research method because it is used in what seem to be exciting studies. However, a mistake which students tend to make is to describe the ins and outs of the actual investigation, especially in studies which are a bit risqué. For example, some students can write pages and pages about Laud Humphreys's study *Tearoom Trade*. However, examiners do not really want vivid descriptions of what men do standing in brown paper bags in public toilets, they would rather know what the results of the study mean for participant observation as a research method. So beware.

Related questions

1 'What participant observation lacks in reliability it makes up in validity.' Discuss.

2 'Non-scientific research techniques such as participant observation have no place in sociological research.' Evaluate this statement.

3 How far is it true to say that participant observation is the only research technique which gives us a true picture of the social world?

To what extent is it possible to apply the
methods and procedures of natural science to
the sociological study of society?

Tackling the question

Questions which ask about the scientific nature of sociology are fairly common. However,
some students tend to find this topic difficult. You need to consider whether sociology
can be studied in the same way as natural sciences. The topic is no more difficult than any
other topic in sociology. Don't be put off by the terms 'science' or 'natural science'. You
don't have to think scientifically to answer this question.

Answer

Guidance notes

Most would agree that one of the aims of science is to measure
phenomena using systematic, objective methods which are free
from personal bias. Scientists are interested in discovering
universal laws which enable them to predict future events, for
example, that water boils at 100 degrees centigrade. This enables
universal statements to be made about the phenomenon under
investigation, and allows human beings to manipulate nature to
their benefit. Scientists believe that there is always an order, or
truth, to discover, and that phenomena do not occur randomly.
In other words, there is always a cause-and-effect relationship to
discover.

The opening paragraph gives
a definition of science and
an example from science which
every school child should know.

In their study of society, positivists use the methods established
by natural scientists in their investigations into the natural world.
Positivists argue that individuals react to external social forces,
and that human behaviour can be studied in the same way as
phenomena in the natural world, in that it can be observed, objectively measured and quantified. They argue that statistical analysis
reveals correlations, causes and ultimately laws of behaviour.
Durkheim used scientific methodology in his study of suicide. By
examining suicide statistics, he found a cause-and-effect relationship between external social forces and the suicide rate. This led

This paragraph can be seen
as an extension of the definition
because it links science to
sociological method. It uses
Durkheim's work on suicide to
demonstrate this link. A frequent
mistake that students make in
this type of essay is to write all
they know about Durkheim's
theory of suicide.

Durkheim to conclude that the suicide rate is a social fact. Positivists argue that when scientific methodology is applied to the study of human behaviour, the results lead to the formation of laws on social behaviour. Positivists criticise other methods of social investigation and claim that sociology should always adopt scientific methodology.

This paragraph introduces interactionism. You'll see that this produces balance which will enable you to move up the mark bands.

However, interactionists have criticised the positivist notion that human beings merely react to social forces. Rather, interactionists claim that individuals interpret situations and act accordingly. Interactionists believe that scientific methodology is inappropriate for studying human behaviour as it cannot uncover how individuals experience and interpret the social world. Furthermore, interactionists criticise the positivist idea that sociology should be objective. Interactionists argue that sociologists should explore the subjective meanings which human beings attach to their own behaviour. Interactionists achieve this in their investigations by using participant observation. This is a major method of investigation in interactionist studies and demonstrates that, although sociology can use scientific methods and procedures, it does not do so extensively.

If the positivist method of enquiry was the only investigation open to sociologists, then much social behaviour would remain undiscovered. For example, it is doubtful whether Humphreys could have conducted his study on homosexual activity in male public toilets by using positivist methods.

The work of Popper is vital to the debate about whether sociology can be seen as a science. Therefore, make it your business to have a thorough understanding of his contribution to the debate. You can also use Popper as a critical evaluation of Marx in any essay which includes Marxism. You will always score a mark for this.

Popper claims that it is possible for sociology to be scientific if it follows the methodological procedures of science. However, Popper questions the idea that scientific methods lead to the discovery of absolute truth. According to Popper, nothing can be proved to be completely true: for example, the statement that all swans are white cannot be proved, as there may be a swan somewhere of another colour which no one has seen. Although sociology can apply the procedures of science, it does not necessarily follow that this will lead to the discovery of universal laws of social behaviour. Popper suggests that in order to overcome this problem of validity, sociology should aim to disprove theories and ideas. He argues that many sociological theories are not precise enough to develop a hypothesis that can be proved false, and as a consequence are not scientific. For example, according to this point of view, Marxism is not scientific because Marx did not specify when and under what circumstances a revolution would occur. However, Keat and Urry who work within a realist perspective, claim that Marxism is scientific because it looks at society by examining its underlying structures. Realists believe that there are wide overlaps between the study of natural science and sociology. They argue that both attempt to give an objective analysis of the areas they investigate.

The positivist view and Popper's ideas are dependent on the notion that science is based on objective methods and procedures. According to Lynch, this is not always the case. Lynch carried out an investigation to discover how scientists really act. He found that when ambiguities in their results occur, scientists make assumptions about the results and are likely to interpret them according to their existing knowledge. This is subjective rather than objective.

> What, scientists cheat? Never. I bet you didn't copy anyone's science results in school!

Kuhn also disagrees with the assertion that scientists engage in the objective pursuit of knowledge. He argues that scientists work within a paradigm, which is a set of shared beliefs that scientists hold about the natural world. Kuhn believes that natural scientific knowledge does not exist independently and objectively, but is constructed by scientists within a framework of assumptions. It is produced rather than discovered. Sociology has a number of competing perspectives to explain social life, and consequently no single agreed paradigm; for example, Marxists, functionalists and interactionists all view the social world in different ways, and come up with very different explanations of social behaviour. For Kuhn, sociology is pre-paradigmatic and therefore is not a science.

Anderson *et al.*, writing from a realist perspective, have criticised Kuhn for underrating the disputes which go on between scientists in the world of natural science. Scientists are not always in agreement: for example, take the conflicting evidence and information produced by various scientists about CJD, the human equivalent of 'mad cow disease'. Some scientists claim that it is safe to eat beef while others advise against it.

> The information on CJD is straight from the newspapers. Don't be afraid to apply your own relevant examples. Examiners tend to reward recent examples which are successfully applied to the question. You need to read a serious newspaper regularly to maximise your chances of scoring high marks. CJD is a good example because it's topical. You could just as easily comment on the Shell/Greenpeace debate on the environmental effects of dumping oil platforms at sea, but remember, one example is enough. By the time you sit your exam, there might be other examples in the news which you can apply instead of CJD.

According to Sayer, in the world of natural science there are two categories of study – open and closed structures. Sayer argues that, within a closed structure, all the factors are controllable and measurable, so the results of this study can formulate universal laws. However, this is not the case within an open structure where the variables cannot be controlled and measured with the same accuracy. There may be many areas of science which make up an open structure, for example, seismologists cannot accurately predict when and where an earthquake will occur. Sayer argues that it is impossible for accurate predictions to be made in much of the world of natural science, just as it is impossible to predict human behaviour accurately in society which, like an earthquake, has many variables acting on it. From the realist perspective there

Question 3

are few differences between sociological studies and the investigations of the natural sciences.

The conclusion summarises the positivist versus interactionist debate. Note that it makes references to when the scientific method can and can't be applied to sociology by using the exact words of the question. The essay title was in the form of a question, and demands an answer. Make sure you give one in your conclusion.

In conclusion, what constitutes scientific sociology varies according to the sociologist's values, which are generally governed by the sociologist's theoretical perspective. Although it is possible to apply the methods of natural science to the study of society, it is clear that not all aspects of society can be investigated by scientific methods. It is doubtful whether the application of scientific methods and procedures would lead to accurate information about gang behaviour, for example. Early positivists assumed that crime statistics were generated by scientific methods and procedures, but interactionist studies demonstrate that the picture of the typical criminal which is built up through the manipulation of statistics is a misconception.

General comments

For candidates taking the AEB examination, it is vital that you revise this area of the syllabus because the essay in this or a similar form comes up so often. You could even use the science debate in the evaluation section of your coursework. The science debate will also give you good grounding in understanding Durkheim's work, particularly in relation to his study of suicide. Make sure you pay particular attention to the spelling of sociologists' names. All too frequently, students misspell Durkheim. This certainly does not look impressive to the examiner.

Related questions

1 'The use of natural science methods is inappropriate in the study of society.' Discuss.

2 'Non-scientific studies of society are nothing more than subjective accounts.' Evaluate this statement.

3 Evaluate the claim that sociology is a science.

Is a value-free sociology either possible or desirable?

Tackling the question

This essay is asking two questions at once. The key words in the title are 'possible' and 'desirable'. In order to achieve a high grade, both questions must be answered. Again, balance is the key to success. This just goes to show the importance of reading the question through a few times before you attempt to answer it. Many students panic in examinations and don't read the question through properly. This often results in good students achieving lower grades than they are capable of. Be warned.

Answer

Guidance notes

Value freedom is the notion that sociological research can and should be carried out without the researcher's own views and values intruding into the research investigation. In other words, the sociologist must be neutral, without biases and should not take sides. Value freedom is often associated with objectivity. According to Bierstedt, research is only objective if it is free from 'subjective elements' and 'personal desires'.

This opening paragraph simply provides a brief definition of value freedom. If you can remember a relevant quote or phrase, it always looks good in an introduction. However, if you can't remember a quote, just do what I've done and put down the key words.

The view that a value-free sociology is both possible and desirable is most closely associated with the positivist perspective. According to positivists, value freedom is achieved by following the methods and procedures of the natural sciences. However, this positivist view of an objective and value-free natural science has been challenged by Kaplan who has pointed out that researchers within the natural sciences do not necessarily follow the methodological approach which positivists maintain that natural scientists use.

In this paragraph, I've explained where the idea of value freedom comes from and how it can be achieved. This is an example of setting the scene and acts as a launch-pad into the main body of the essay.

In addition, values must inevitably come into any research whether it is within natural science or social science. As soon as a researcher chooses one subject to study rather than another subject, that researcher has expressed a value. For example, within sociology it is evident that classical sociologists such as Durkheim and Marx, who both claimed to be objective and scientific, were in fact motivated by their own personal values. The Marxist Baritz takes this argument one stage further by saying that the values which form the basis of any piece of research are less likely to be those of the individual researcher than of the organisation or person funding the research. This argument is supported by the example of the Rowntree Trust which funds research into poverty.

Weber is a key name in the value-freedom debate, and no essay on this subject would be complete without him. This is because Weber points to the relative nature of values. You must make sure that you've a good understanding of Weber or your value-freedom essay will be weak and incomplete.

Weber would agree that the values of the researcher do influence the area of study. He pointed out that values are inevitably linked to the society in which the researcher works, so different societies will give rise to different types of knowledge. The knowledge reflects the values of that particular society. For example, the Bulger case has given rise to numerous attempts to link the mass media with anti-social behaviour. Research of this nature is unlikely in a third world country as other issues or values take priority. However, Weber believed that once the topic of investigation had been chosen, objectivity was possible, providing the researcher does not make any value judgements upon the results of the research.

This paragraph uses information from another area of the syllabus, in this instance, health, and applies it to the question. This is a useful technique to learn and requires a bit of bravery and forethought on your part. This just goes to show that a little knowledge can go a long way.

According to Marxists, the researcher may consider the results to be value-free but there is no guarantee that others will look at the results of the research in the same manner. Marxists would argue that some research findings can be used to benefit the dominant social class. Additionally, the powerful can commission research to suit their own purposes; for example, the layout of large supermarket chains is designed by social scientists in order to maximise profits. Where research findings do not fit in with the goals of the body funding the research, the funders have the power to suppress the findings. This occurred in the case of the Conservative government which commissioned *The Black Report* and *The Health Divide* which were research investigations into the health of the nation. The results showed that bad health was linked to inequalities between the social classes. The government did not publish these reports as they might have proved damaging to Conservative policy.

Gouldner is another essential theorist in the value-freedom debate. You will notice that the introduction of Gouldner takes the essay in a different direction. The contemporary issue of homelessness is used to support

According to the American Marxist Gouldner in his essay 'Anti-Minotaur: The Myth of a Value Free Sociology', just as the mythical creature the Minotaur cannot be separated into man and bull, neither can values be separated from facts in sociology. Gouldner argues that the whole idea of a value-free sociology stems from the self-interest generated by capitalism. He claims that early American sociologists who had been critical of

American society came under attack from those in power and as a result began to lose their academic status. In order to save themselves, they created the myth of a value-free sociology and were no longer critical of American society. However, Gouldner claims that 'sitting on the fence' and saying nothing critical about society is in itself a value, so a value-free sociology is not possible. He argues that if something is wrong in society, sociologists have a moral duty to speak out because silence concerning a social inequality is as good as support for social inequality. For example, sociologists should comment on people living and sleeping on the streets, and if they stay silent about it, then they are as good as saying that people should live and sleep on the streets. Gouldner believes that sociology is not and should not be value-free.

Since the 1960s, many modern sociologists have rejected the notion that a value-free sociology is either possible or desirable. The interactionist Becker claimed that as the social world was mainly seen through the eyes of the powerful, sociologists should attempt to redress the balance by showing the social world through the eyes of the underdog. Hence, many pieces of research from the second half of the twentieth century have not been value-free, nor have they attempted to be. This trend was encapsulated in Parker's work *View From the Boys*, which shows crime from the point of view of those who commit it.

Marxist sociologists would go further than Becker by advocating a form of sociology which is clearly political and therefore not value-free. Marxist sociology not only looks at the structured inequalities of the social world, but it frequently gives a prescription to remove these inequalities as it perceives them to be immoral. This idea that sociology is political and therefore not value-free is not exclusive to left-wing writers. For example, the New Right have infiltrated the world of sociology by applying right-wing explanations, laden with right-wing values, to the causes of social problems: Marsland criticises the Welfare State for creating a culture of dependency and advocates the destruction of the Welfare State as we know it. Many sociologists concur with Gouldner in believing that sociology is not and should not be value-free.

In conclusion, it appears that contemporary sociology has lost its infatuation with value freedom. Most contemporary sociologists do not see a value-free sociology as either possible or desirable. It has been accepted that values which are present in every society will become part of the socialisation process of any individual. This in itself will ensure that a value-free sociology is impossible. Those like Marsland who attack sociology for its left-wing bias are themselves guilty of their own right-wing bias through their preoccupation with maintaining the present capitalist social order.

Gouldner's argument. Can you think of different examples which equally demonstrate Gouldner's point? You need to develop the confidence to apply theoretical debates to contemporary issues. It will make your essays more enjoyable to read and write and will show that you can make the link between theory and practice.

The conclusion refers to, and answers, the question. It also makes further reference to why a value-free sociology isn't possible. Note that the question has been answered at various points in the essay and not just in the conclusion. Regular reference ot the question will keep your essay tight and to the point.

General comments

Essays on value freedom are fairly clear-cut – there's a limited number of ways in which the examiner can ask the question. Therefore, unlike other essays, it's highly unlikely that you'll have trouble in interpreting the question. However, do give yourself time to read the question thoroughly and plan your answer carefully. Unlike other areas of sociology, where there are any number of theorists who can be applied to explain a point, freedom has some specific theorists who must be used, namely Weber and Gouldner.

In addition, as stated in the guidance notes, don't be afraid to link in other areas of sociology. In the case of this essay the subject of health has been linked with the subject of value freedom. The modularisation of A-level Sociology has encouraged students to view each topic as a separate subject. It's important, however, to recognise the interrelationships between all subjects on the syllabus.

Related questions

1   To what extent can value judgements be kept out of sociological research?

2   'There is no such thing as value neutrality in sociology and it is therefore pointless to pursue it.' Evaluate this statement.

3   How far is it true to say that values inevitably enter into any piece of sociological research?

Question 5

'Sociologists have largely ignored the negative aspects of family life.' Discuss.

Tackling the question

This essay title represents a new trend in questions on the family. In the past, essay questions have typically focused on the evolution of the nuclear family and have neglected negative aspects of family life. However, a careful examination of evidence shows that not all sociologists have ignored negative aspects of family life. Weak candidates typically agree with the essay title and focus on the inadequacies of the functionalist perspective of the family. However, strong candidates will use either critical theory, that is dark-side theory, or feminism as a critique of functionalism. Both of these theories explore the negative side of family life. Questions like this one can mislead students, so be careful.

Answer

Guidance notes

In the past, the dominant perspective in sociology was functionalism. Functionalists such as Murdock attempted to identify a relationship between the family and other parts of the social system, like the economy. It has been argued by many opponents of functionalism that in the pursuit of identifying the relationships between the family and other areas of social life, functionalists have focused on the positive aspects of family life while ignoring the negative aspects, such as domestic violence and child abuse. Critical theorists have focused on the negative side in an attempt to refute functionalist theories. This essay will demonstrate that, while functionalists have ignored some aspects of family life, critical theorists have not.

According to Murdock, who writes from a functionalist perspective, the family serves four basic functions which contribute to the maintenance of the social system. These functions are sexual, reproductive, educational and economic. In support of Murdock it is true to say that if there were no sex or reproduction the human race would cease to exist. Murdock also claims that the family plays an educational role in that the home is where, in

> Following the introductory paragraph, the essay goes straight into functionalist theory. I've set Murdock and Parsons up as straw men, with the purpose of knocking them down later.

the first instance, children are socialised into the norms and values of society. For Murdock, the family's economic function is based on a specialised division of labour. In Western societies this usually involves the man taking on the role of breadwinner while the wife's fundamental role is that of houseworker and childcarer. Murdock argued that this specialised division of labour based on co-operation between husband and wife is functional for the individual as it provides 'rewarding experiences' for the spouses working together. He sees the specialised division of labour as positive and ignores the tensions that it can bring to many relationships.

Murdock's notion of a specialised division of labour providing rewarding experiences for spouses has been criticised by feminist sociologists. According to Ansley, the specialised division of labour often causes conflict and can result in domestic violence.

A more concrete example of Murdock's failure to deal with the negative side of family life becomes apparent when his depiction of sex and reproduction is examined. Murdock argued that sex plays a functional role for individual members of the family as well as a functional role for society as a whole. He claimed that spouses have rights of sexual access to each other and that sex effectively strengthens family bonds. Murdock suggested that sex unites couples and that the 'feel-good factor' that sex creates between husband and wife filters down to other family members.

> I think you'll agree that Morgan's quote is quite easy to remember.

However, Morgan has criticised Murdock's depiction of family life, saying that 'Murdock's nuclear family is a remarkable institution where the husband and wife have an integrated division of labour and a good time in bed'.

> Even though I've criticised Murdock, the use of the word 'nevertheless' quickly allows me to change the direction of the essay back to functionalism and the introduction of Parsons' work. Murdock and Parsons are essential in this essay because they have in the past been influential writers on the family, and have both ignored the negative side of family life. The exclusion of these two theorists is equivalent to building a house and forgetting to lay the foundation stones.

Nevertheless, Murdock's work has been supported by the writings of another functionalist, Parsons. Parsons argued that the family serves two 'basic and irreducible functions'. The first function of the family is to socialise children. Parsons claimed that primary socialisation involves two processes, firstly, the internalisation of society's norms, values and culture, and secondly, the structuring of the personality. The second function of the family is to stabilise adult personalities. Parsons suggested that the emotional security that the couple provide for each other acts as a counterweight to the stresses and strains of everyday life which can lead to unstable personalities. He argued that, in modern day Western society, adults are largely isolated from their wider families and that, as a result, the spouses learn to depend on each other for emotional support. Parsons then took this one stage further and suggested that the close interdependent relationship between man and wife means that the couple can act out their childish whims within the relationship. He argued that this allowed the couple to recharge their batteries while giving emotional support to one another.

However, Parsons has been heavily criticised. Like Murdock, Parsons has been attacked for idealising the family and focusing on the positive aspects of family life at the cost of the negative. In a similar way to Murdock, Parsons sees the family as a place of harmony with well-adjusted children and parents who cater for each other's every need. Parsons and Murdock both stand accused of ignoring domestic violence and child abuse which are so common that they are statistically normal.

According to the critical theorist Leach, the family is 'the source of all our discontents'. Leach refutes both Murdock's and Parsons' unrealistic picture of the family. He argues that 'the emotional stress between the husband and wife, and parents and children, is greater than most of us can bear'. Leach goes on to say that the family is a place where 'the parents fight and the children rebel'. Leach is supported by the work of Laing, who argues that many children are subjected to violence and violation of their rights by their parents. Laing claims that this can negatively affect the emotional development of the child. For Laing, contrary to the functionalist argument, the family can be dysfunctional for many individuals.

Dobash and Dobash further criticise the functionalist view of the family. They argue that functionalists ignore the fact that many families have a dark-side. This is supported by the early work of Giddens who argues that 'the home is the most dangerous place in modern society'. Supporting Giddens' claim are the facts that women are more likely to be beaten or raped within the home by a partner than by a stranger on the street, and that children are more likely to be sexually abused by a relative than molested by a stranger. The official statistics for domestic violence suggest that one in eight women are physically abused by their partners. The official statistics for domestic violence are based on reported cases only. Many women do not report their violent partners and as a result many instances do not become statistics. Women's Aid have suggested the higher figure of one in six women who face violence in the home. Cooper argues that the unequal power relationship within the family effectively gives the man the right to hit his wife.

In conclusion, it appears that functionalist sociologists have largely ignored the negative aspects of family life, and as a result

After some basic criticisms of the two functionalists, I've used the work of critical theorists to evaluate the work of Parsons and Murdock, and address the fact that not all sociologists have ignored the negative side of the family. Note that the essay changes direction about mid-way through. This acts as an indication that I've achieved a balance between those who ignore the negative side of family life and those who don't. This takes careful planning and practice. If you do not plan your essay carefully, you may find that after 45 minutes you only have half an essay which doesn't really reflect what you want to say.

I've included some supporting evidence here in the form of statistics for domestic violence. I've mentioned the fact that this is likely to be a gross underestimation of the true extent of domestic violence in order to give food for thought. It's OK to do this in your essays, but remember, don't go off at a tangent. Try to stick to the issue. You may like to think about the reasons why these statistics are an underestimate. You'll be able to use this information in essays which look at the validity of statistics, e.g. crime statistics, or positivist studies of society.

Remember, your conclusion needs to reflect that some sociologists have ignored the negative side of the family, but others haven't. Summarise the points, and if you can, make some sort of statement or comment about the dark-side of the family. Sometimes it pays to get down off the fence in a conclusion.

Murdock and Parsons are accused of producing an inaccurate portrayal of family life as it is experienced by many individuals. Their view of the family tends to be through rose-tinted glasses and neglects real-life experiences of violence and abuse. Although the family may be functional for society, it is not necessarily functional for individual family members. By portraying family life as harmonious, and seeing domestic violence within the home as abnormal, it can be argued that the functionalist view can effectively 'keep women in their place'. However, feminist sociologists and critical theorists such as Leach and Laing have not neglected the negative aspects of family life. Critical theorists in particular have sought to address the 'dark-side' of family life. Although functionalists have ignored the negative aspects of family life, it is not true to say that all sociologists have neglected this important issue.

General comments

Students tend to find this type of essay easy to write because it is so nitty-gritty. Most people have an opinion about domestic violence and child abuse because they are emotive issues. In addition, most people know someone who has been affected by the negative side of family life. Anger can make for good, even passionate, essay-writing. However, you must not get carried away by emotion in your essay. This may seem like a hard-faced comment to make, but some students have tackled this essay from a very personal level, and while I would agree that people have a right to get angry about things that they've experienced, an essay is not the place to divulge harrowing personal accounts.

Related questions

1   'Functionalists have ignored the dark-side of the family.' Discuss.

2   Evaluate the claim that 'the home is the most dangerous place in modern society'.

3   'The family is a haven in a heartless world.' Evaluate this claim.

Question 6

Explain and evaluate the contribution of feminists to an understanding of the family.

Tackling the question

At long last examiners are beginning to ask questions about feminist perspectives in sociology. This essay requires both an explanation and evaluation of the contributions of feminists to an understanding of the family. It's important to note the word 'feminists' – plural. This is a useful clue as to what the examiner is looking for – it indicates that there is more than one feminist theory to consider. It's also important to remember what the term 'evaluate' means in A-level sociology. It means that you need to produce both supporting and contradictory evidence for the topic or issue under discussion. Remember to be as critical as you can.

Answer

Guidance notes

There are several competing feminist perspectives which attempt to understand family life and, in particular, the role which women play in this social institution. While there are similarities between the different schools of feminism (most feminists would agree that women are oppressed within the family) there are also some stark differences: on who benefits from the domestic division most, and how these inequalities can be rectified. This essay will examine three competing feminist perspectives on the family – liberal feminism, Marxist feminism and radical feminism.

From the outset the essay spells out that there are several feminist perspectives to consider. It also tells the reader that there's some competition between the various perspectives. The fact that there are three perspectives to explore makes the essay easy to structure – a section of the essay must be given to each.

Liberal feminists have pointed to the family as the key source of male domination and female oppression. They point to the fact that in the past, fathers have had the right to rule other family members. This right is enshrined in tradition, custom, and even law, like 'the rule of thumb', which in the past gave a husband the right to hit his wife with an implement, such as a stick, as long as it was no wider than his thumb. Liberal feminists such as Gavron have argued that the family is a patriarchal institution which mirrors patriarchal society. Just as women tend to be subservient in the workplace, so they tend to be subservient in

In this paragraph, I offer an explanation of liberal feminism. The example of the 'rule of thumb' brings a historical look at women's lives to life. There are other examples that you could use in place of this one. Did you know that in the past a husband could put a face harness on his 'nagging' wife? The harness had a spike attached to it which rested on the woman's tongue. The husband then had the right to lead his harness-wearing wife through the town for everyone to see. Remember that whichever example you choose to use, one is enough, and be brief.

the home. Gavron points to the facts that women are over-represented in jobs which revolve around cooking, cleaning and caring, and that women in paid work are still likely to have a male boss. Liberal feminists believe that patriarchy is not a physical force, but a force of institutional control.

According to liberal feminists, the law can be used to rectify these gender inequalities and when parity exists in wider society, it will eventually follow that parity will exist within the family. However, this view can be criticised because changing the law is a very slow process. Furthermore, changes in the law which have been designed to promote gender equality in society, such as the Sex Discrimination Act 1975, have been viewed by many as ineffective. Evidence suggests that women are still paid less than men and have fewer chances of promotion in the workplace.

In this paragraph, I've introduced the Marxist feminist perspective as a critique of the liberal feminist approach. Some students find the Marxist feminist approach particularly difficult, especially Benston's explanation of how the family is linked to capitalism. I've broken this argument down into four key points so that it becomes a little easier to understand.

Marxist feminists reject many liberal feminist ideas. According to the Marxist feminist, Benston, patriarchy is a form of exploitation and oppression of women which is generated by capitalism. Benston argues that the traditional division of labour within the home benefits capitalism in a number of ways. Firstly, it is cost-effective to capitalism, in that if women did not carry out housework and child-rearing tasks, the family would have to pay for these services. This would increase the family's expenditure and would consequently result in higher wage demands. Secondly, women provide a reserve army of labour which can be accessed at times of national crisis, as, for example, during the Second World War when women went into the factories to work in the place of men. Thirdly, in their caring capacity, women prepare men for work: they cook, they clean and are there to gratify their husbands sexually. Women meet all the needs of men, which ensures that their husbands are fit and healthy for work; this therefore benefits capitalism. Finally, because men have a financial obligation to their families, they may be dissuaded from taking industrial action.

I bet you never forget Ansley. Like the essay before, I've used the example of domestic violence to explain a point. This just goes to show that the same example can be used in a variety of topics. You should also note that this paragraph doesn't just explain the Marxist feminist position, it also spells out their solution to female oppression.

Benston is supported by Ansley who argues that women in their supporting role are like 'sponges' which absorbs the frustrations and anger of their husbands caused by working within the capitalist system. Rather than the husband taking his anger out on his boss, he is likely to take it out on his wife. Ansley goes further by referring to housewives as 'takers of shit'. Further support for Benston comes from McAfee and Wood who argue that the relationship between husband and wife is often no more than 'petty dictatorship'. This argument is supported by the rising incidence of reported cases of domestic violence. Statistics indicate that one in eight women experience domestic violence at the hands of their husbands. It is important to note that these statistics are only based on reported incidents of domestic violence – the true figure for this type of abuse is likely to be much higher than the statistics suggest. According to Women's Aid, the real statistic for domestic violence is more likely to be one in six. For Marxist feminists, this exploitation of women in the home can only end when capitalism is overthrown and replaced by a new epoch of socialism.

According to Barrett and McIntosh, Marxist feminists can be criticised for ignoring family diversity. Marxist feminists assume that all families consist of a mum, dad and children: they ignore other family forms such as single-parent families.

Just a quick criticism to separate Marxist feminism and radical feminism.

An alternative feminist perspective on the family and marriage is put forward by radical feminists. Whereas Marxist feminists argue that capitalism is the main beneficiary of the traditional division of labour within the home, radical feminists argue that it is men who benefit first and foremost. The radical feminists Delphy and Leonard argue that the family has a central role in maintaining patriarchy. Women are oppressed by men and this oppression stems from unequal labour relations within the home. Delphy and Leonard argue that there are two roles within the family. One role is the head of household, and this is usually taken by the male. The other role is that of a 'dependant'. This role is usually taken by the wife who is at least semi-subordinate and owes her husband obedience and respect. The wife has responsibility for domestic, sexual and emotional labour. According to Delphy and Leonard, women perform on average 57 household tasks which their husbands benefit from, e.g. cooking, cleaning, nursing. Oakley offers similar evidence. She found that women spend more than 70 hours a week doing housework.

I've introduced the radical feminist perspective as a critique of Marxist feminism before going on to explain their own position. You may like to write your own list of tasks that you think women perform for the benefit of men. See if you can come up with 57 tasks like Delphy and Leonard. My students came up with fewer than 20. See if you can do any better. You should note that in this paragraph I've applied the work of Oakley to support Delphy and Leonard. Remember, the objective of your essay is to show the examiner your knowledge and understanding of a subject, and how well you can apply and evaluate information.

Functionalists like Willmott and Young would not agree with the radical feminist position, or indeed any feminist perspective of the family. Willmott and Young's research suggests that the family is becoming more symmetrical. One would think then that in cases where the male is out of work and the female is working that some form of rôle reversal would have taken place. Delphy and Leonard point to research which was conducted in Port Talbot where the men had been made redundant. They found that even though the men were home all day they still did very little in the way of housework. For Delphy and Leonard, these men were still benefiting from the traditional division of labour within the home despite the fact that they were no longer the breadwinners. This evidence suggests that it is not capitalism which benefits most from the traditional division of labour, but men. More supporting evidence comes from a similar study conducted by Mckee and Bell who also found that role reversal had not taken place within the household.

Delphy and Leonard, like Benston, can be criticised for ignoring family diversity. Furthermore, their work is based on unrepresentative data. Many studies, including the research by Bott, have found that there is more equality in terms of the domestic division of labour within middle-class families. Delphy and Leonard's data from their Port Talbot research may have had an in-built bias towards their theory because they chose a sample from a working-class area. In other words, they knew that their results would 'fit' their theory.

As this essay has shown, feminist contributions to our understanding of the family do have similarities. However, the feminist perspectives which have been examined differ in their 'solution' to female oppression in the home. Whereas liberal feminists believe that inequality within the family can be ended by changes in the law which will create a change in attitude towards women in general, and Marxist feminists argue that only a change in epoch will end inequality within the home, the radical feminist Shulamith Firestone has argued that 'woman will never be completely free until reproduction has been taken away from the womb'. With the recent developments in 'cloning', this may not be as far-fetched as first thought. Meanwhile other radical feminists have argued that women will not be free until they turn to lesbianism.

> I don't think you could get more radical than Shulamith Firestone (or Shula Shaker as she was affectionately known by my students last year).

In conclusion, feminist perspectives have moved sociological research away from the previously male-stream sociology of functionalists. Feminist perspectives have highlighted the negative aspects of family life which have previously been largely ignored. In addition, feminist perspectives show how the inequalities of society as a whole are mirrored within the family. Overall, feminist perspectives have provided sociology with a more complete picture of family life and how it is experienced by many women.

> Not only does the conclusion summarise the feminist perspectives on the family, but it manages to have a little dig at male-dominated sociology.

General Comments

This essay is quite complex as it requires an explanation and evaluation of three different feminist perspectives. However, this did mean that the essay was largely self-structuring. The information covered may well prove useful in other essays: for example, the Marxist feminist explanation of the relationship between the family, work and the capitalist system can be applied to essays on work and stratification. The information on violence within the home can be used in support of dark-side theorists. Meanwhile, the radical feminist explanation can be used in an essay on symmetrical families or conjugal roles, as well as in essays which explore the occupational situation of women.

When writing essays, try to include a good mix of contemporary examples to support what you're saying. Not only will this make the essay more enjoyable for the reader but it will help you to remember some key points when it comes to revising for the examination.

Related questions

1   Compare and contrast two competing feminist perspectives on the family.

2   Assess the view that the fundamental role of the family is supporting the needs of capitalism.

3   How far have feminists contributed to our understanding of the family?

Question 7

Discuss the suggestion that the family has become more symmetrical.

Tackling the question

This essay is a favourite with most students, so why is it that so many students score low marks on this topic? The key, it seems, is in evaluation. I think that, in general, the information that is required for an essay on the symmetrical family is relatively straightforward. Many students then fall into the trap of producing a piece of work which is heavy on description and light on evaluation. Most of my students score higher on essays which they perceive as hard than on essays which they see as easy. I think that the motto of this story is don't be fooled into thinking one essay is easier than another, and never get too complacent about your answer. Every essay you write will be judged on the same criteria of knowledge and understanding, application and evaluation.

Answer

The opening paragraph sets the scene – it sums up the supporting evidence for symmetrical families, and tells the reader who first introduced the term 'symmetrical family'. If you do this, you will be showing off your knowledge from the outset. You'll notice that, in this opening paragraph, I've told the reader what I'm actually going to do in the essay. Some students find this a good technique to adopt. The introduction becomes a brief essay plan which can be used to keep you on the right lines.

Notice how this second paragraph launches straight into Willmott and Young's evolutionary theory

According to recent media hype, the 1990s has given birth to the phenomenon of the 'new man'. This suggests that men are now doing more housework and childcare, while women are increasingly selling their labour in the labour market, and consequently contributing economically to family life. Willmott and Young predicted that the family, in its third stage, would become more symmetrical. They claimed that the family would evolve from an institution based on patriarchy and a specialised division of labour, to one characterised by equality and democracy. This essay will conclude that, although relations within the family may have changed, the new man syndrome is nothing more than an exaggerated myth.

Willmott and Young argue that the family has evolved through three different stages – pre-industrial, industrial and symmetrical. They argue that the early industrial family played host to a specialised division of labour whereby the adult male sold his labour in the labour market in exchange for a wage, while his wife became primarily responsible for childcare and housework. In comparison, the symmetrical family is described as an institution in which the partners play more equal roles. This suggests that the family has evolved from having gender-segregated roles to joint conjugal roles. Willmott and Young claim that this third stage of evolution would see men contributing to housework and child-care, while women would increasingly become engaged in paid employment, thus contributing to the economic needs of the family.

Willmott and Young's suggestions can be supported by changes in the occupational structure. Over recent years there has been a decline in the traditional industries, such as mining, and a rise in white-collar, office-based work, such as administration. Many women have taken up both part-time and full-time paid positions in offices. These changes in the occupational structure demonstrate that women are no longer confined to the home, and are playing a more active role in providing for the family's economic needs.

However, according to Rapoport and Rapoport, even though women are increasingly taking up paid employment, there is no indication that the family is becoming more symmetrical. They argue that the wife's career is often seen as secondary to her role as a housewife and mother, and that the wife's working hours revolve around family commitments. Delphy describes how the modern family is far from symmetrical. She argues that family life is still largely based on patriarchy and inequality, and claims that women who have careers are often blamed for problems in the family. Recent evidence suggests that working women are to blame for their children's poor academic performance. This does not offer much support for the claim that the family is becoming symmetrical. Women are still made to feel ultimately responsible for their children's welfare and emotional development while working men tend to escape from such criticism.

Willmott and Young's research is questioned by Oakley. Oakley carried out a survey of 40 housewives and found that housework is still regarded as a woman's job. According to Oakley's research findings, women spend on average over 70 hours a week performing household chores. This would suggest that there has not been any real convergence of the social worlds of men and women. Evidence demonstrates that even women who work full-time are still predominantly responsible for housework.

Maynard points to two sorts of empirical evidence which contradict Willmott and Young's notion of the symmetrical family. Firstly, American time-budget studies show that because women are contributing to housework and taking paid work, their working week has actually increased. The women who have the

of the family. Get this out quickly and accurately: it can become so boring if you drone on and on.

By the time you're a third of the way through the essay you should have offered some supporting evidence and launched into your first attack on the notion of symmetrical families. This paragraph is rich with evidence contradicting Willmott and Young. Consider who does what in your own family, and compare this with the division of labour in your grandparents' day. You could even do a small-scale survey by asking all the adult males you know about the last time they cleaned the toilet. Don't forget to check their answer with their partner's. You may be surprised how many lies you get told!

Introduce empirical evidence when you get the opportunity – it makes the case you are building much stronger.

longest working week have husbands who have the shortest working week. Secondly, Maynard points to British studies which show that housework is still based on a sexual division of labour. Maynard supports Oakley's findings that the idea of the symmetrical family is a myth.

Oakley's findings are also supported in the work of Mckee and Bell, who carried out a survey in Kidderminster which looked at potential role reversal situations. Mckee and Bell investigated situations where the husbands were unemployed (due to redundancy) but their wives remained in full-time paid work. Mckee and Bell wanted to see if role reversal had occurred as a result. They found that despite the fact that the husband was at home all day while the wife worked, in the majority of cases the women still performed most of the household chores. In similar research carried out in Port Talbot, Delphy and Leonard found that men did not take over the domestic chores because they perceived it as an attack on their masculinity. Delphy and Leonard also claim that when men do perform housework, they see it as 'helping' their wives and do not tend to take any personal responsibility for it.

It's important not to be one-sided. Make sure that you offer critiques of all the theorists, not just the ones you disagree with.

However, Oakley has been criticised on methodological grounds. She only interviewed 40 housewives, and it could be argued that the sample was too small to be representative of the whole population of married women, so it is difficult to make generalisations from her findings. Similarly, the research carried out in Kidderminster and Port Talbot was looking at the effects of redundancy and employment on the family. Both pieces of research were conducted in working-class areas and were about working-class families. It could be that the research findings are only representative of the working class. Indeed, according to research by Bott, middle-class men do carry out domestic chores. However, Rapoport and Rapoport dispute the work of Bott. They cite a study which looks at the family life of managing directors and claims that many middle-class families are less than egalitarian. In some instances the wife plays a central role in securing business deals by hosting dinner parties and generally being an appendage on her husband's arm. In many middle-class families, the husband is dominant and dictates to his wife and children. Consequently, Rapoport and Rapoport claim that many middle-class families are less than egalitarian, and the claim that they are more symmetrical than working-class families is a myth.

Research conducted by the organisation Mintel offers some support for Willmott and Young's ideas, in that it suggests that men are actively taking part in the domestic sphere of family life. However, the research takes just one regular chore a week as indicating that men are playing an increased role in housework. This could mean as little as doing the washing-up on Sunday, so the research which suggests that men are doing more around the house needs to be regarded with caution. In addition, it should be considered that what men say they do around the house and what they actually do is not always the same thing.

Further evidence which challenges Willmott and Young's notion of the symmetrical family comes from Edgell's analysis of decision making within the family. Edgell's study of middle-class families found that there was a clear imbalance of power between husband and wife when important decisions which affect the whole of the family were made. Edgell claimed that the husband tends to have greater influence over important decisions by virtue of his economic dominance. In other words, because the husband tends to earn more, he plays the dominant role. This refutes the notion of the symmetrical family. Edgell is supported by Bernard, who claims that in many instances women perceive themselves as the inferior partner in a marriage. Bernard also claimed that many women feel the need to apologise if they feel they have been bossy but they accept this as an unchallenged characteristic of their husbands. Bernard concludes that while women feel inferior to men, the family cannot be considered egalitarian.

Don't just focus on housework as an indication that the family is not symmetrical. By using Edgell, I've taken the emphasis off housework and put it on decision making. This gives your essay more balance and depth.

An increase in the number of reported cases of domestic violence suggests that the contemporary family is not more democratic and equal. The official statistics for domestic violence suggest that one in eight women are subjected to violence at the hands of their partners. This statistic is only based on the reported cases of domestic violence and is an underestimate of the true extent of violence within the home. According to Dobash and Dobash, power differentials in the family give rise to domestic violence, and as a result of their power, men regard it as their right to hit and reprimand their wives. This does not suggest that the family is symmetrical, because the person with the biggest fists, or the most violent temper, tends to win.

Another essay in which the example of domestic violence is used to make a point. This shows how versatile one example can be.

In conclusion, it appears that despite Willmott and Young's prediction that the family would become more symmetrical, the contemporary family is far from democratic and equal. Evidence suggests that women are still predominately responsible for house-work and for childcare. Meanwhile men are still dominant in areas such as decision making. Domestic violence remains the strongest evidence against the notion of the symmetric family, with challenges to male authority often ending in bruising or even broken limbs. The notion of the 'new man' can largely be seen as a myth.

If you can, make a statement at the end of your essay. I would be very surprised to see a student sitting on the fence on this one.

General comments

As long as you can offer breadth and depth in your answer, you can easily score high marks for this essay. Although housework is a key issue in the symmetrical family debate, it's not the only issue. Make sure that you don't neglect other important aspects such as decision making and domestic violence. There is alternative evidence which can be used to challenge Willmott and Young which I didn't use in this essay, namely the research on men's participation in childcare. However, be aware that there's a vast amount of information which can be used in an essay such as this. You must select the information you're going to use very carefully. In an examination it would be easy to write for three hours about the symmetrical family; in reality you only have 45 minutes. If you go over time, you may do less well on other essays. Plan your answer carefully and make sure you answer the question. Don't write all you know about a subject – be selective with your information and concentrate on writing a high quality essay.

Related questions

1   'The new man is a modern-day fairy tale.' Discuss.

2   How far is it true to say that the division of domestic tasks is still unequal in modern society?

3   'Although relationships within the family are constantly changing, women's contribution to housework remains the same.' Evaluate this statement.

Question 8

Evaluate the notion that the family is a dying institution.

Tackling the question

Although this essay seems straightforward enough, beware that you do not fall into the classic trap of producing an uncritical response. Weaker candidates tend to respond uncritically to the essay title by pointing to evidence of the rising divorce rates, the increase in the number of single-parent families and the number of couples choosing to remain childless. Stronger candidates will use this information but will supply evidence which contradicts these findings. Good students will be able to present an argument which suggests that the family is adapting rather than dying.

Answer

Guidance notes

In contemporary British society, recent governments (both Labour and Conservative) have claimed that the family is in decline. Politicians, social commentators and the mass media have pointed to a number of indicators which, it is claimed, show the family to be under threat. Their evidence tends to take the form of increasing divorce statistics, the rise in the number of single-parent families, the number of individuals who are choosing to stay single, the number of individuals who are choosing to stay childless, the rise of homosexual/lesbian families, and the apparent increase in child abuse. On the other hand, many sociologists have argued that the family is not a dying institution, rather that the structure of the family, and ideas about family life, are changing.

In the opening paragraph I sum up the 'dying institution' debate. This tells the reader that I'm writing an essay worthy of the higher mark band from the very start.

The notion that the family is a dying institution is dependent on the definition of the family which is used. The functionalist Murdock claimed that the family is 'a social group characterised by common residence, economic co-operation and reproduction. It includes adults of both sexes, at least two of whom maintain a socially approved relationship, and one or more children, own or adopted, of the sexually cohabiting couple'. In other words, the

A definition of the family is always a good place to start. This paragraph sets Murdock's definition up in order to knock it down again in the next paragraph. Murdock is easy to criticise. Last year my students used his definition to see if they belonged to a family. Only a quarter of the class did. The other three-quarters of the class were most put out because they felt that they belonged to a family yet fell outside Murdock's boundaries.

This paragraph provides an historical account of the changes in the divorce law and explains how this has affected the divorce rate. Note how reference is made to the question. If you do this in your essay you'll find that it keeps you on track. In the following paragraph, I bring the divorce law right up to date.

family lives together, pools its resources, the male and female adults have sex together, and reproduce. The sexual relationship between the adults has to be one which is socially acceptable in the society in which they live. Murdock assumed that the nuclear family which he described is universal. This means that it exists in this form in every society. It is clear that if Murdock's definition of the family is used, the institution of the family does indeed appear to be dying, as, for example, more and more people appear to be choosing to stay single and childless. Recent evidence has shown that relatively young women are choosing to be sterilised before they have ever had children in order to follow a career.

However, Murdock's definition has been heavily criticised for being too narrow. According to this definition, a single parent (through death or divorce) or a child of a single parent, does not belong to a family. Similarly, if the children have left home, then the parents that are left no longer constitute a family. Nevertheless, Murdock's definition of a family is widely accepted, and deviations away from his prescriptive family have been seen as indications of the death of the family.

The most prominent indicator which suggests that the institution of the family is dying is the rising divorce rate. Evidence shows that in 1961, 32,000 divorce petitions were filed. By 1988 this figure had dramatically increased to 183,000. According to *Social Trends* (1993), since 1971 the divorce rate in Britain has doubled. There has been a change in general attitudes towards marriage which has been reinforced by changes in the law. The Divorce Reform Bill (1969) which came into force in 1971, made divorce easier. The most dramatic rise in the divorce statistics came soon after this law was passed. Some criticised the law for encouraging the break-up of families while others welcomed the law which saw the end of many unhappy 'empty shell' marriages. Similarly, the divorce statistics rose dramatically in 1985 shortly after the introduction of the Marital and Family Proceedings Act 1984, which legislated that a divorce could be sought after just one year of marriage. Some see the law as paving the way for the death of the family.

However, the last Conservative government introduced legislation which demands that when a marriage breaks down, individuals must attend mediation sessions and show that they have lived separately for a year before they can apply for a divorce. This was a weak attempt at trying to preserve the institution of the nuclear family.

According to functionalists such as Parsons and Fletcher, the rise in the divorce rate stems from the fact that marriage is becoming increasingly valued. The explanation for this paradox is that individuals tend to idealise the idea of marriage and consequently demand a lot from it. Parsons and Fletcher argue that if individuals feel that they are not getting the experiences which they think they should be achieving, they are inclined to end a marriage which might have been perfectly acceptable in the past.

Oakley puts forward an argument which suggests that the changing role of women has affected the divorce rates. Oakley claims that some women who have entered the labour market are now economically independent. She argues that women in this position are able to leave an unsatisfactory marriage because they are no longer financially dependent on their husbands. Furthermore, Oakley is supported by Hart who suggests that many working women have had to take on the dual role of wage earner and houseworker. Hart argues that the dual burden of being an economic provider and the subservient houseworker can lead to tension between the husband and wife and, in particular, lead to the female partner petitioning for a divorce.

The work of Hart and Oakley is used to support the notion that the family is a dying institution. Remember that, providing the information is linked in properly, even supporting evidence constitutes an evaluation.

At first glance, the increase in the divorce rate does imply that the family is a dying institution. However, there has been a trend towards what sociologists call 'serial monogamy', where divorced individuals remarry. Evidence suggests that remarriage is likely to occur after a short space of time. Serial monogamy gives rise to the reconstituted family, which is a family made up of step-children and step-parents. According to Duncan and Rodgers, for the majority of children, living life as a member of a single-parent family is fairly short-lived. It has been argued that when a marriage breaks down, it is the partner who is being given up, not necessarily the idea of marriage and family.

This paragraph and those that follow challenge the assertion that the family is a dying institution. This gives some balance to the answer. It's important to remember that if a question asks you to discuss or assess a proposition, this is because it is not a cut-and-dried issue. To write strong essays, make sure you challenge assertions and evidence.

It has also been argued that the increase in the number of individuals choosing to live together is an indication that the family is a dying institution. According to statistics, young people are living together for longer periods than they did in the past, but most established cohabiting couples do end up getting married eventually. Wicks criticises the notion that cohabitation is a sign that the family is a dying institution. He claims that around 30% of couples who live together have children out of wedlock. Furthermore, Chester claims that cohabiting couples tend to marry once they have had children. Therefore it can be argued that the increase of divorce and cohabitation is not an indication that the family is dying, but rather an indication of the change in attitudes towards marriage and family life. Indeed, most unmarried couples with children or single-parent families would be appalled to be told that they do not constitute a family.

Nevertheless, evidence does show that more individuals are choosing to live alone. According to *Social Trends* (1993) in 1971 just over 6% of adults lived alone. This figure has now doubled. This would suggest that fewer people are craving family life and are following different paths, for example, many individuals are choosing to travel and/or focus on a career. However, this may not be an indication that individuals are rejecting the idea of having their own family. Many individuals are choosing to settle down at a later stage in life. Just because someone lives alone when they are 30 does not mean that they will necessarily be living alone when they are 35.

Some commentators have pointed to the increase in the number of reported cases of child abuse to demonstrate that the family is a dying institution. Indeed statistical evidence of child abuse and domestic violence contradicts the functionalist view that the family is 'a haven in a heartless world'. Abuse, either domestic violence or child abuse, has been going on for centuries; it is only recently, however, that abuse has been put on the social agenda and become a socially acceptable subject for discussion. Indeed, many soap operas have used the issue of child abuse in their story lines, and this may to some extent have encouraged individuals to come forward and report what has happened to them. It is doubtful if there has been any real increase in the amount of abuse; it is merely that more abuse is being reported. It is difficult therefore to use this as evidence that the institution of the family is dying.

The concluding paragraph summarises the two opposing arguments and the evidence. Note that I've brought in the controversial Child Support Agency and made a statement about its possible effects on the family. It's OK to bring in other issues at the end: it gives food for thought. However, remember not to go overboard. Try to remain detached and impersonal. The conclusion also mentions that most people tend to aim for the ideal of marriage. Find out how many of your classmates anticipate being single at the age of 40. I bet it's not many.

In conclusion, the notion that the family is a dying institution is dependent on the definition of the family used. If Murdock's definition is used, then the family he describes does appear under threat. However, Murdock's definition of the family is very narrow and does not take into account alternative family structures, like single parents and gay families. It appears that there has been a change in the structure of the family and a general change in attitudes towards family life. However, this is not an indication that the family is dying; it is merely adapting. Evidence suggests that cohabitation for many eventually leads to marriage and many divorced individuals eventually remarry. Individuals still aim for the ideal of marriage and family life. It will be interesting to see if the introduction of the Child Support Agency acts as a deterrent to separation and divorce. This could result in dire consequences for individuals in unhappy marriages, especially those affected by violence if the violent partner refuses to leave for financial reasons.

General comments

To score highly for this essay you must go beyond a description of the divorce rates and the number of single parents currently living in Britain. You must try to be critical of the proposition that the family is a dying institution. If you're revising the topic of the family, it is crucial that you know Murdock's definition of the family and the associated criticisms.

Related questions

1 'Despite viable alternatives, the nuclear family is still the dominant family structure in Britain.' Discuss.

2 Evaluate the notion of the conventional family.

3 'Most families are made up of a father, a mother and two children.' To what extent is this statement a true picture of the family in modern British society?

Examine sociological accounts of 'new vocationalism'.

Tackling the question

As new vocationalism is a fairly new debate in sociology, it's one which the textbooks don't tend to have a great range of research about. In order to answer questions on this topic thoroughly, you'll have to go beyond most textbooks. In particular, you should look for information on GNVQs as this is the area which it's essential to cover in order to make your essay contemporary. An essay which just looks at Youth Training is less likely to achieve a top grade.

Answer

In this introductory paragraph I've given some of the history of new vocationalism. In doing this, I've explained what new vocationalism means and the type of courses it includes. Defining your terms always makes a good start in any essay.

The term 'new vocationalism' describes the view that education should primarily meet the needs of the economy. This stems from the notion that young people are ill-prepared for work because they have limited work experience, and as a consequence are not looked on favourably by potential employers. New vocationalism was introduced in Britain to give young people work experience via different forms of training. The early forms of Youth Training involved paying trainees £25 a week to take part in a scheme. This was to encourage employers to take on trainees as it did not cost them anything. The government claimed that young people were unemployable because they lacked work skills and experience. The introduction of new vocationalism required a number of educational policy changes including the introduction of Youth Training Schemes (YTS) and more recently, General National Vocational Qualifications (GNVQ). Early sociological accounts of new vocationalism have tended to examine Youth Training, as this scheme pre-dates GNVQs.

In this paragraph, I've introduced one of the earliest accounts of Youth Training. Note how it only

One of the earliest sociological accounts of Youth Training comes from Finn, who claimed that Youth Training was introduced to reduce the number of young people who were registering as unemployed. He argued that making young people go on Youth Training Schemes reduced the unemployment statistics, and made the government's performance look better. This appears to be a valid criticism, as the government introduced a policy which meant that those on Youth Training Schemes were not included in the unemployment statistics even though they did not have a permanent full-time, appropriately paid occupation. The government proposition that young people were unemployable because they lacked work skills and experience was, according to Finn, simply untrue. Various studies from around Britain support Finn's contention that school leavers are workwise. For example, part-time work, although predominantly taken by women, is also taken by young people in full-time education, as many teachers of 15–19 year olds can testify.

The introduction of Youth Training Schemes was unpopular among many, especially the young, as it was viewed as 'slave labour' whereby the young person did the same job as other employees but received only a fraction of the pay. For others the introduction of such schemes has lead to greater unemployment. Why would employers take someone on for a fair wage when they can get a young person do to the job at no cost to the company?

offers an account of Youth Training. You must be aware that this is only a partial account of new vocationalism. The essay needs much more than this to address the question thoroughly.

The work of Clarke and Willis also lends credibility to Finn's arguments. Clarke and Willis claim that young people are kept in 'suspended animation' when they enter new vocationalism. This means that they are kept on ice until work becomes available. Philip Cohen's study of Youth Training Schemes also supports Finn. Cohen claims that the view that youth unemployment is the result of young people's lack of training is false. His study shows that the training on many Youth Training Schemes does not give young people skills for work. Instead they are taught 'behavioural etiquette' whereby they learn that if they fail to get a job it is their own fault through their 'failure' to sell themselves adequately.

The studies mentioned so far have put forward pessimistic accounts of new vocationalism. This is mirrored to a certain extent by the work of Roberts. Roberts' study shows that although Youth Training recruits from all levels of academic ability, it has little credence as a qualification. This is because, according to examination results at age 16, the majority of youth trainees come from the bottom half of the ability range. This in itself undermines the credibility of Youth Training as a qualification because the label attached to Youth Training is that it attracts low ability youth. It does not really matter how successful individuals have been on a scheme, they may still be perceived as having low ability.

This paragraph provides supporting evidence for the work of Finn. Note that the two accounts of new vocationalism which have been given have been negative.

Question 9

The application of Roberts' study of Youth Training starts to give some balance to the essay because it shows that there are some Youth Training places which are worthwhile. In addition, it shows that not all Youth Training schemes are the same. It's important to have balance in your essays. You'll not score highly without it.

This paragraph starts to look at GNVQs. If your school or college has GNVQ courses, try to find out the retention rate of the students – you could use this information in your essay either to confirm national trends or to deny national trends.

However, Roberts distinguished three types of Youth Training. Firstly, 'sponsored' Youth Training, where the employer takes the best qualified youth and there is a virtual guarantee of a job at the end of a period of quality training. Roberts recognised that this type of Youth Training had higher status than other types and was in fact worthwhile. Youth taken on under this scheme were known as apprentices rather than being labelled as trainees. An 'apprentice' is generally seen as having a higher status than a 'trainee'. The second type is 'contest' Youth Training where firms take on more trainees than needed. The trainees then have to compete with each other throughout their training period and at the end the best trainees are kept on. Finally, he cites 'warehousing', which tends to be found in areas of high unemployment. This type of scheme takes youth with the lowest qualifications and offers little opportunity for permanent employment. According to Roberts, on this type of scheme 'trainees literally mark time'. Thus according to Roberts' view, some types of new vocationalism are more exploitative than others. Roberts' study has more merit than some other studies of youth training as he distinguishes different types of Youth Training.

The introduction of GNVQs has meant that young people now have an alternative to Youth Training. GNVQs offer young people the chance to study a vocational area at an academic level. However, this type of course has received bad publicity. The statistical evidence suggests that many GNVQ students fail to complete their courses, and the GNVQ retention rate is problematic for most further education colleges. In addition, a distinct gender divide has already appeared between GNVQ programmes. For example, most applications for GNVQ Health and Social Care come from young women.

Some institutions and employers question the academic credibility of GNVQ Advanced as an alternative to A-levels. Traditional redbrick universities still tend to opt for students with A-level qualifications. Likewise, many job advertisements still demand the traditional GCSEs and A-levels. The first complete study of GNVQs has recently been published by Wolf and lends support to these arguments. Wolf's study argues that GNVQs do not have the same academic status as A-levels. In addition, like Roberts' study of Youth Training, Wolf found that GNVQs were not effective as a pathway to work. Furthermore, a study by the London School of Economics shows that in terms of earning power, Advanced GNVQs, although theoretically equivalent to two A-levels, are only worth the same as five good GCSEs.

However, new universities are starting to look favourably on GNVQ students, recognising that the students' skills of self-directed study equip them well for undergraduate study. Nevertheless, in 1996 only 5% of GNVQ students applied for higher education places but 96% were made offers by higher education institutions. In comparison, around 85% of A-level students made applications to higher education institution and around 90% were made offers.

In conclusion, sociological accounts of new vocationalism have generally been negative. Only Roberts has offered a wide analysis of Youth Training, singling out 'sponsored' schemes as worthwhile. Despite his findings, even Roberts concludes that the best way to occupational success is via an academic route. However, Roberts' colleague, Moore, believes that new vocationalism has won the ideological battle with traditional liberal education. At present the recruitment policies of employers and traditional universities support Roberts' account of new vocationalism, but the fact that new universities are welcoming applications from GNVQ students supports Moore. Nevertheless, it appears that the GNVQ has many battles ahead in the quest to be seen as a real alternative to the A-level.

> This conclusion refers to the question and mentions both major types of new vocationalism. Note how the conclusion sums up the arguments and makes a comment on the future of GNVQs. This is a good way of finishing an essay – it provides a definite ending.

General comments

Answers which rely solely on sociological explanations of Youth Training are likely to result in poor marks. Some of your classmates may have come to A-levels through the GNVQ route, or may be taking an A-level alongside a GNVQ qualification – ask them about their experiences. Those of you who are taking a GNVQ course could relate your own experience to this essay. However, remember not to make the essay too personal. You have to try and remain objective.

Related questions

1 To what extent have sociologists maintained that there is a relationship between education and the economy?

2 How far is it true to say that new vocationalism will give young people the skills required for employment?

3 'New vocationalism hides the true extent of youth unemployment.' Evaluate this statement.

Explain and account for the differences
in educational achievements between the
social classes.

Tackling the question

The reason why some children from working-class backgrounds do not do very well in education has puzzled academics and politicians for years: as a result there is a lot of research on this topic. Consequently, one of the problems that students sometimes have with this essay is what information to leave out and what information to keep in. The answer is to offer a variety of studies from a range of perspectives. This approach to tackling sociology questions is more likely to put you in the higher mark bands. Examination boards frequently instruct their examiners to keep candidates who offer a limited range in the bottom bands.

Answer

The first paragraph gives some fairly recent (at the time of writing) data which does two things. It shows that, in general, the higher a child's social class the more likely that child is to succeed in education, but it also shows the reader that your essay is based on up-to-date information. However, you should remember that this information will not be up to date for long. It's up to you to keep up with new findings. Note that the opening paragraph also maps out the essay and tells the reader what material is going to be used.

The term 'differential educational achievement' refers to the differences in academic attainment between social groups. In this essay it refers to the differences in educational achievement between social classes. The difference between the achievement of children from working-class and middle-class backgrounds is generally expressed in numerical form. In other words, by positivist data. For example, evidence from *Social Trends* (1994) shows that 32% of those with degrees had fathers with professional backgrounds (professional is one category in the occupational class structure which indicates middle-class occupation), whereas only 3% of degree holders had fathers who were unskilled manual workers (unskilled manual is one category in the occupational class structure which indicates working-class occupation). Sociological explanations for these differences in educational attainment between social classes tend to fall into two broad groups: those which look at material and cultural factors, and those which look at the effects and organisation of schools. This essay will examine each of these explanations in turn.

Material deprivation has long been recognised as a factor in differential educational achievement. The National Children's Bureau's longitudinal study, which examined all children born in England in one week of March 1958, found that a significant number of children experienced material disadvantage in the form of poor housing and low income. This was also found by Douglas in his longitudinal study of 5000 children. Douglas commented that when housing conditions are unsatisfactory, children score badly in academic tests. More recently, Halsey *et al.* have shown that economic hardship is a major obstacle to educational success.

In a similar vein, other research has pointed to the importance of cultural factors to educational achievement. Sugarman claimed that the subcultural attitudes of the working class account in part for the working classes' general lack of educational success. In particular, Sugarman argued that the working-class preference for immediate gratification – that is, the desire for enjoyment straightaway – means that the working-class child is more likely to leave education as soon as legally possible to take up employment.

However, there are two major problems with this argument. Firstly, when Sugarman was writing it may have been common for working-class children to be forced to leave school as soon as possible in order to bring money into the home of a disadvantaged household. Sugarman does not explore this in his analysis of the educational achievement of social classes. Secondly, in contemporary British society there seems little point in any child leaving education early as there are very few employment opportunities for young people.

Douglas has also contributed to the cultural deprivation theory of differential educational achievement. He claimed that the most influential factor in a child's educational attainment was the degree of parental interest in each child's education. Douglas's research revealed that middle-class parents showed more interest than their working-class counterparts.

However, Douglas's measure of 'parental interest' can be criticised on grounds of validity. Douglas measured parental interest by measuring the number of contacts the parents had with their child's school. He found that middle-class parents attended more school functions than working-class parents. In some instances school functions, such as sports days, are held in the day-time, when many working-class individuals are in work. It can be argued that it is far easier for individuals in white-collar work to negotiate time off work to attend such events; many blue-collar workers do not have the same luxury. Similarly, parents' evenings tend to be held in the evening at secondary schools, and many working-class parents work shifts and cannot get the time off to attend such events. Douglas's measurement of parental interest

This is a simple, even obvious, statement that material factors play a part in educational success. You might try to think of something from your own experience to support this part of the argument, e.g. did your school have a fund to help some pupils go on school trips?

The work of Douglas on 'parental interest' is popular with students. Some try to get a whole answer out of it – don't fall into this trap. You really need to apply more recent work, such as Ball *et al.* This will demonstrate to the examiner that you have a wide range of knowledge which you can apply to the essay title.

is therefore open to criticism. Furthermore, as Blackstone and Mortimer point out, the middle-class nature and atmosphere of the school could deter working-class parents from attending events. They argue that middle-class parents are more comfortable in the middle-class atmosphere of the school. A failure to attend school events is not necessarily an indication of lack of interest. Many working-class parents actively encourage their children towards educational success as they see it as a route to occupational and economic success. In many instances working-class parents want their child to have things which they did not have, or were lacking in their own childhood. Furthermore, it could be added that if a child constantly misbehaves in school, the parents of that child are likely to visit the school more often than any other parents, regardless of social class.

Be warned again: Bernstein is popular with students. You need to make your essays stand out from those of other students. This doesn't mean that Bernstein shouldn't be used to answer this question, but don't spend any length of time on him.

Bernstein contributed to the cultural deprivation theory by pointing to the language differences between the middle class and the working class as a factor in differential educational attainment. Bernstein made the distinction between elaborated linguistic code and restricted linguistic code. According to Bernstein, the academic success of middle-class children may be achieved because they can use the same elaborated linguistic code as teachers. In comparison, working-class children are disadvantaged in school because they tend to use the restricted linguistic code which is not used in schools.

Notice how Labov is used as an evaluation and a link into the interactionist perspective.

Labov, who uses an interactionist approach, provides a useful evaluation of Bernstein's work. His work with black American children shows that language is not necessarily a key factor in differential educational achievement. Labov demonstrated that social situation determines language and that the code used by the black working-class children he came into contact with was just as sufficient for educational success as the code used by middle-class children.

Some students start to become a bit sentimental when they write about the interactionist perspective on education. Some see it as a conspiracy by 'evil' teachers who deliberately label 'poor' working-class kids as ' less able'. Beware, this is not the interactionist argument! Remember that interactionists

The inadequacies of the above theories have led other sociologists, particularly interactionists, to look at the organisation of the school itself and the teacher's role in an attempt to explain differential educational achievement between the social classes. Rist pointed to both of these factors in an attempt to explain differential educational achievement. In a study of an American kindergarten, Rist noted that the teacher had divided the children between different tables according to their perceived ability, which tended to be related to the social class of the children. Becker's study of Chicago High School teachers reached similar conclusions. Teachers labelled middle-class students as more able. Both these studies show that teachers evaluate their students in terms of non-academic criteria, such as appearance, rather than ability. This labelling can have effects on educational achievement. Rosenthal and Jacobson's experiment in a Californian elementary school showed the possible effect on academic attainment of the self-fulfilling prophecy. The experiment involved informing teachers that a particular group of students were 'spurters', and that they should expect those students to come along in leaps and bounds in the near future. When Rosenthal and Jacobson followed up the study, they found that the students who they singled out as 'spurters' had indeed improved in terms of their academic ability. Rosenthal and Jacobson put this down to the effects of labelling. This means that the expectations of teachers are conveyed to students, shaping their self-image. They then perform accordingly.

Interactionist studies also explain differential educational achievement between social classes by reference to the organisation of the school. Like Rist and others, Keddie's study of a comprehensive school revealed a relationship between perceived ability and social class. Working-class children tended to be in bottom streams and middle-class children tended to be in the top streams. In addition, Keddie discovered that those in the bottom stream were denied sufficient knowledge for examination success. The recent introduction of tiered GCSE examinations means that students entered for some subjects at foundation level cannot possibly achieve the pass grade of 'C' because the maximum grade available is 'D'.

Despite the fact that interactionist research offers valuable insights into differential educational achievement between social classes, labelling and self-fulfilling prophecy cannot on their own provide an adequate explanation. Fuller's study of black female students in a London comprehensive school showed how the girls refused to accept negative stereotypes and worked hard in order to gain academic success. In addition, Peaker estimated that the effect on educational attainment of teaching was only about a third that of home factors.

Finally, in a society where educational failure is just one of many structured inequalities, it is inevitable that some will fail. Almost 30% of those candidates sitting A-level Sociology will fail. The real explanation for failure is that it is built into the educational system and therefore inevitable.

look at the meanings and interpretations that individuals put on the behaviour of other individuals. If you were an infant school teacher with a labourer's child and a doctor's child, who would you expect to get the highest qualifications? The moral of this story is: don't label interactionists as the pupil's friend!

Here the conclusion does not use any of the previous studies to explain differential educational attainment, but shows that failure is inevitable with a pass/fail system. Ending an essay with something new is another style that you could adopt.

Question 10

General comments

The relationship between education and social class is a common question which can come up in a variety of forms – teachers' expectations, the organisation of the school, home backgrounds and self-fulfilling prophecy are all trigger words for this type of essay. The essay content will remain much the same, but the information must be applied in different ways. Try to keep abreast of new research in this area. You'll need to up-date my examples on a yearly basis. *Social Trends*, and periodicals such as *Sociology Review* are useful resources, as is the *Guardian's* educational supplement on a Tuesday and the *Times Educational Supplement* (your school or college library should have these).

Related questions

1 'As far as educational achievement is concerned, what happens at home is far more important than what happens at school.' Discuss.

2 Assess the importance of background factors in determining educational success.

3 'Teachers' expectations are of vital importance in educational success.' Evaluate this statement.

Evaluate the argument made by some
sociologists that the education system acts as a
mechanism for role allocation.

Tackling the question

Many students will find this a 'hard' question because they will have difficulty in understanding what the essay requires. In reality, it's a fairly straightforward question once you know and understand the term 'a mechanism for role allocation'. When translated, all it means is that education sorts out 'clever' pupils from 'thick' pupils and that 'clever' students will end up with the best jobs – doctor, dentist, architect – while the other pupils end up with what's left.

Answer

Education can be seen as serving purposes other than the obvious one of providing children with knowledge: one of these is to act as a mechanism for role allocation. This means that education is a kind of sieve which allots individuals to their occupations within the economy according to their abilities. In other words, those with the most talent will be allocated the most functionally important jobs in society. The view that there is a relationship between education and the economy is often associated with the functionalist perspective. More recently, it has been associated with the 'New Right', which emphasises individualism and the notion of the free market economy. The claims of functionalists and the 'New Right' have been countered by both liberals and Marxists. This essay will examine these views in some detail.

The introduction explains what a 'mechanism for role allocation' means. Without a defination the essay will not make sense.

According to the early functionalist Durkheim, education is a mechanism which transmits society's norms and values to children. Durkheim argued that through the teaching of history, school-children learn a sense of patriotic belonging to 'their' country.

Parsons, also writing from a functionalist perspective, expanded on Durkheim's work. Parsons made a distinction between the ascribed status and achieved status of individuals. Ascribed status was something that stemmed from within the family and was fixed at birth; for example, a child can be the first or last born of the family and consequently has the status of youngest or eldest. This status is fixed and cannot be changed. However, achieved status is different, and is not fixed. Rather, Parsons argued, achieved status is earned in wider society; for example, hard work at school can lead to a child becoming a doctor in later life. This status is earned through hard work and educational achievement.

At this point I've used the example of SATs and League Tables to illustrate the functionalist argument. You could refer to whatever merit system your school used to reward pupils for good work. One of my local schools awards 'good pupils' with a McDonald's voucher and £2 off a school trip to Alton Towers!

According to Parsons, schools promote the value of academic achievement by rewarding pupils for their 'good work'. In this way pupils will strive to become high academic achievers. Parsons claimed that primary schools ranked children according to their ability and that secondary schools took this a step further by sorting pupils into those who would leave school early and go directly into work, and those who would benefit from further and higher education. In this way, schools play a part in role allocation. The notion that education is competitive was reinforced by the New Right philosophy of the last Conservative government, which to a large degree mirrored the functionalist perspective. The Conservatives emphasised competition between pupils by introducing Standardised Assessment Tests (SATs) which enable comparisons to be made between pupils, and indeed between schools on a national level via League Tables.

The Davis and Moore argument is probably the most important part of the functionalist approach. If your institution does not teach stratification you would be well advised to read up Davis and Moore in your textbooks. Don't just look at their work in the education chapter – you need to read about them in the stratification chapter to develop a better knowledge of their ideas.

The functionalists, Davis and Moore, see a more direct link between the education system and the world of work. According to Davis and Moore, education sieves individual pupils according to their ability. They argue that the pupils with the most academic ability receive the highest academic qualifications, and this in turn leads them to occupy the functionally most important jobs in society. Davis and Moore argue that these jobs have the highest rewards in terms of both status and money. Thus they claim that education is a mechanism for role allocation.

However, the functionalist claims put forward by Davis and Moore can be criticised. It is doubtful if education can measure pupils in terms of their abilities. At present, the most common measurement of abilities used by the education system is examinations. These only measure a narrow range of abilities, and candidates that are successful have been judged mostly on their ability to remember information and their ability to succeed under examination conditions, rather than on other criteria.

A further criticism of Davis and Moore is that their claim that those with the highest qualifications will receive the greatest occupational rewards in terms of earnings and high status is open to question. In the United Kingdom some of those with the highest qualifications are people with doctorates who work in the Higher Education sector yet they do not necessarily receive high financial rewards. Similarly, it can be argued that some drug dealers receive massive earnings yet they have low status and their position is certainly not functional to society. Further attacks can be made on Davis and Moore's notion that the functionally more important jobs in society attract higher financial rewards and high social status. It can be argued that a refuse collector is more functionally important to society than a top medical consultant. Consultants may save hundreds of lives in their lifetimes, but the refuse collector potentially saves society from diseases. The consultant serves the needs of individuals while the refuse collector serves the needs of whole communities.

In addition, the liberal view of education can be used as a critique of the functionalist view. The liberal view does not see the purpose of education as a mechanism for role allocation but as a means for individuals of all ages to develop their full potential. However, as Moore has pointed out, the binding of education more tightly to the economy seems to have become the dominant ideology throughout the 1980s and 1990s. This development fits in better with the functionalist approach.

If the functionalist view is correct and individuals can obtain achieved status through education, then this should lead to an open society where individuals can move up and down the class system. If Britain a were meritocratic society – one where individuals are rewarded or given merit for their achievements – there would be some movement in the British class structure. However, successive studies of social mobility have shown that this is not the case and that there is little serious cross-class mobility. The studies show that individuals tend to stay in the same social class as the one in which they were born.

This section introduces evidence from another part of the syllabus, social stratification. The best essays tend to link other parts of the syllabus to the subject under investigation. Weaker students tend to view each topic area as a separate entity. Try to get out of the habit of putting particular studies into single pigeon-holes. So much knowledge goes unused if you do this.

The Marxists Bowles and Gintis argue that the major role of education is the reproduction of labour power, whereby individuals from the higher social classes have a greater chance of attaining an occupation with high status and high reward than those individuals from lower social class groupings. This argument is confirmed in the case of British society by the Oxford Mobility Study's *1:2:4 Rule of Relative Hope*, which shows that a boy from the working class has four times less chance of achieving a well-paid job in the service class than a boy who is born into the service class.

Furthermore, Bowles and Gintis argue that there is a very close correspondence between the social relationships within the education system and the social relationships in the workplace. They argue that the function of schools is to produce workers with the kinds of attitudes and behaviour which will be beneficial for work under capitalism. Bowles and Gintis claim that the hidden curriculum teaches pupils obedience, subservience and motivation by external rewards, and teaches them to say 'yes sir/miss' or 'no sir/miss'. They argue that school effectively prepares individuals for taking passive roles in the workplace where they will have to obey their managers and work for cash rather than job satisfaction. Bowles and Gintis see education as preparing individuals for their role in later life and it is therefore a mechanism for role allocation, since the majority of pupils from comprehensive schools are taught to be subservient, while pupils who attend exclusive public schools, such as Eton, are taught to be leaders.

Bowles and Gintis also provide a range of positivist data which undermines the functionalist arguments. They show that there is no relationship between intelligence (as measured by IQ tests) and income, and that there is no relationship between academic qualifications and income. However, they do demonstrate that there is a relationship between an individual's sex, race and class at birth and that individual's income. Thus, the idea of a meritocratic society can be rejected.

In the concluding paragraph I've offered a final evaluation of both the functionalist and the Marxist approaches to role allocation. I've ended by pointing to an alternative area of research for educationalists to consider. There is nothing wrong with concluding with a suggestion, as long as it fits the topic.

The Marxist explanation of the role of education highlights the weakness of functionalist accounts, but it too has its inadequacies, some of which it shares with functionalism. Both perspectives see individuals almost as puppets of the social system with the individual's life controlled by unseen social forces. British capitalism had a subservient workforce which had been sifted into appropriate occupational routes long before compulsory education came into existence in the last century. Contemporary sociologists would be better occupied in looking at how the education system can differentiate between those who are able to work and those who are destined to experience unemployment.

General Comments

As with all essays, this one demands a good knowledge and understanding of the material associated with role allocation and education. The material would also prove useful in answering questions on recent education reforms. You could also apply some of this information to questions on new vocationalism. In order to develop a greater understanding of this topic, you'll need to read the relevant section in the stratification chapter of your textbook. This will make the Davis and Moore argument clearer to you and help you improve your essay technique.

Related questions

1 'The education system is alleged to provide a ladder of opportunity, but in reality it maintains the status quo.' Discuss.

2 To what extent have sociologists maintained that there is a relationship between education and the economy?

3 How far is it true to say that education is merely the servant of the capitalist class?

Question 12

Assess the main sociological arguments for differences in educational attainment between the sexes.

Tackling the question

Recent evidence shows that females now do better in education than males and sociologists anxious to explain this phenomenon. In the past, males achieved higher qualifications than females throughout the education system. This was reflected in sociological research. There is a wealth of sociological information which explains male success. However, the new evidence of female success has left sociology short of studies which explain it. As a consequence most A-level texts have little information on female educational success. Many students try to answer gender and education questions based on old evidence. In order to keep up-to-date with new developments in sociology you should make sure that you read periodicals such as *Sociology Review* which document the latest research.

Answer

This introductory paragraph gives some of the historical background to the battle of the sexes in education, but it also shows that educationalists like Blackstone were aware of the changes in the 1980s. Note how the paragraph introduces evidence by referring to the general trend at GCSE level rather than to exact percentages. The examiners do not expect you to remember precise numerical details.

Until recently, evidence suggested that from secondary school age onwards males were more successful than females in education. They passed more examinations and achieved higher grades. However, evidence has demonstrated that in the past females were discriminated against in education. One example of this discrimination can be seen by looking at quota systems. Evidence shows that if entrance examinations to mixed grammar schools had been on test scores alone, two-thirds of the places would have been occupied by females because at the age of 11, females tend to do better than males. However, in order to have a balance of male and female pupils, some grammar schools increased the pass mark for female pupils but lowered it for male pupils. Similarly, girls wanting to read medicine at university would have unknowingly faced the barrier of a 20% limit on female candidates. In the mid-1980s, Blackstone pointed to the myth of girls' under-achievement at school. Blackstone is supported by recent events which show that girls get better GCSE results and better A-level results than boys. Evidence also shows that the proportion of women progressing to higher education is now higher than the proportion of men. Sociologists have attempted to explain why females are now out-performing males in education. This essay will explore their contrasting views.

Some would argue that innate ability explains the differences in educational achievement between the sexes. An experiment by Molfese and Molfese, which was carried out on babies who were one week old, showed that female babies have a superior innate language ability to that of male babies. However, superior educational achievement may not solely be the result of biological differences between the sexes. Many sociologists point to the different socialisation processes which males and females encounter as an important aspect of the differences in behaviour between males and females.

According to Norman, pre-school conditioning and sex stereotyping mean that girls and boys have learned different outlooks and skills by the time they start school. This may affect their performance within school. A study by Murphy and Elwood shows that the choices children make at an early age lead to differential educational attainment between the sexes. They claim that at the playgroup stage, boys tend to use construction toys or bikes, whereas girls tend to use pencils and scissors. Murphy and Elwood argue that boys are more active while girls tend to be more passive, and this may be due to what the children have already learned about the appropriate gender role. Murphy and Elwood suggest that by the time children get into reception classes, boys may already be disadvantaged in learning writing skills because they are not as experienced as girls at using pencils. They claim that during their time at school, boys and girls develop different styles of writing and these are influenced by the types of books they read. Girls eventually develop descriptive and narrative skills which translate into superiority over boys in GCSE English.

Note how this paragraph starts to give sociological explanations in a chronological sequence by referring to what happens before school, in the playgroup and so on. This technique, where information is put in chronological order, can be used in other answers. It can enhance the coherence of your work.

The differences between male and female reading skills have been highlighted by a number of other studies as an influential factor in explaining the differential educational achievements between the sexes. Downes has argued that linguistic factors are crucial in education. His study shows that boys play sports and computer games whereas girls tend to read. He argues that boys' relationships with other boys revolve around 'doing' activities, whereas girls' relationships with other girls are based on talking. Downes suggests that boys perceive reading as an unsuitable activity. The difference in reading aptitude has been highlighted by studies in both Britain and America.

This paragraph refers to the different patterns in leisure activities between boys and girls.

However, Norman, Murphy and Elwood, and Downes can be criticised. If these commentators were correct, then girls would always have achieved higher education attainment than boys. None of these writers explains the shift from males doing better to girls doing better and their explanations of differential achievements can therefore be refuted.

Eccles' study of American children claims that the influence of parents outweighs other factors contributing to differential educational attainment between the sexes. Her study revealed a number of differences in the ways in which parents treated their child according to sex. She argued that parents tend to spend less time reading to boys and buy their sons fewer books, and that they tend to spend more time with their sons on outdoor pursuits. Eccles also suggested that girls spend more time in sedentary, that is non-active, pursuits. According to Eccles, these factors advantage girls in school.

The research by Wragg shows support for Eccles' study in the previous paragraph. It gives the examiner evidence of cross-cultural comparisons.

Wragg's research on British children also shows that reading is an important factor to the higher educational attainment of girls. According to Wragg, three-quarters of children aged five to seven are regularly read to by their mothers. In comparison only half of this group of children are read to regularly by their fathers. In addition, most infant school teachers and classroom assistants are women. It may be that boys come to view reading as a feminine activity. Wragg conducted an experiment which involved fathers reading to their sons. Wragg found that once this started to occur, the boys' reading scores improved.

This evaluation concerning socialisation patterns emerged in an informal class discussion. Remember you can learn from other students in your group.

Both Eccles and Wragg have argued that socialisation plays a major part in explaining the different educational achievements of the sexes. However, the socialisation patterns whereby girls learn the skills necessary for educational success have existed for a number of years, yet it is only recently that females have outperformed males in terms of educational attainment. Neither Eccles nor Wragg addresses the shift from male success in education to female success in education.

Alternative explanations for female success in education may lie in changes in the wider society. Some sociologists have suggested that equal opportunity initiatives have helped females improve their educational attainment. However, Measor and Sykes believe that equal opportunity has had a limited impact on the whole of the education system because only a minority of schools have implemented an active equal opportunities programme. They do not believe that equal opportunities explain the shift from male educational success to female educational success.

According to Sammonds, white lower-working-class boys are the lowest achievers in education; equal opportunities policies have done very little for them. However, Harris *et al.* claim that the attitudes of these boys towards academic goals account for their relative failure. Researchers (such as Willis) have shown that lower-working-class males have traditionally had negative attitudes to educational success. It is important to look at the changing attitudes of females towards education.

Changes in the opportunities for women to work coupled with ideological changes may explain the recent educational success of females. Evidence shows that two out of three women are now in the labour force and this is likely to increase in the next century. There has also been the rise of feminism, which may have helped to shape female attitudes towards education. Many women will now encourage their daughters to have a career and work hard at school in order to achieve, whereas previously, as Douglas points out, parents have been more concerned with the educational success of their sons. This is because, in the past, it was expected that females would marry and have children soon after leaving school and that their husbands would cater for their economic needs. Thus, changing ideas about the female role may have helped shape female attitudes towards education, leading to the educational success of females.

This paragraph is not using sociological research, but it is applying sociological ideas to the question. You might attempt to apply a Marxist analysis to the question. This is a really useful skill to work on.

According to Sharpe, the 1990s have seen a change in the attitudes of working-class girls. Sharpe claims that, unlike in the past, the majority of females to whom she spoke did not want to leave school at 16; rather, they wanted to progress into the sixth form or college. Most of Sharpe's sample of girls were aware of the importance of careers and knew that they should stay on in education as long as possible in order to maximise their potential in the job market.

Past research which tried to explain the under-achievement of girls, such as Spender's work and Stanworth's study, showed that discrimination against girls by teachers and schools may have been explanatory factors. More recent research by Younger and Warrington makes similar claims to explain boys' under-achievement. They argue that boys' subjective experience of education may be particularly important. They cite fifth-form boys who complained that the girls in the class got more attention from male teachers. However, the same study saw boys as lacking in concentration. The lack of male concentration in class was also cited in Downes' research. It could be argued that, as a result of past studies which showed that teachers paid less attention to the female members of the class, teachers have consciously sought to redress the issue by giving attention to the girls in the class. The majority of teachers going through teacher training may well be familiar with the early work of Spender and Stanworth. Perhaps their research has brought about a reverse of the self-fulfilling prophecy.

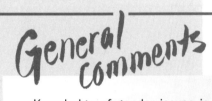

In conclusion, it is probably the case that sociological explanations which explore wider social change are more adequate than those which look at differences in the socialisation of young girls and boys. It is certainly the case that in modern British society more women are in paid work. It is also the case that there has been a rise in single-parent families, the majority headed by women. It could be that these women are acting as a positive role model for the younger generation of females who are achieving more than males in terms of educational attainment. It is possible that it is a change in women's consciousness that has triggered their educational success.

General comments

Knowledge of gender issues is often essential to answer questions on education. Sometimes, examination boards ask general questions on educational attainment and the best answers will refer to class, gender and ethnicity. The old research on gender and education, for example Spender and Stanworth, is still sometimes called for in education essays. One way in which examiners do this is to ask questions about research based on classroom observations.

Related questions

1   To what extent is it true to say that changes in wider society have led to a general increase in the educational achievement of females?

2   Evaluate the idea that boys' under-achievement in education is a result of the socialisation process.

3   'Boys who under-achieve in education have only themselves to blame.' Discuss.

Question 13

Examine the notion that technology is the major determinant of alienation at work.

Tackling the question

Mature students tend to find essays on work and leisure easier than students in the 16–19 year old age group. This is because mature students may have first-hand experience of alienation within the world of work. However, most 16–19 year olds have part-time jobs. If you have a job, how much freedom do you have to make decisions? My guess would be that most individuals have felt alienated at some point in their lives. Once in this frame of mind, this essay will become much easier for you to understand.

Answer

There is no agreed definition of the term 'alienation', although most contemporary sociologists take it to mean a 'lack of satisfaction at work'. The term was first used by Marx who originally used it to describe the experience of workers under the conditions of capitalism. In the 1960s, Blauner used it in his study of work. His definition of alienation referred to the objective conditions of workers (the kind of technology used at work), and the subjective feelings of workers (the way that the workers actually felt about their work).

Blauner examined four different types of technology; craft work, machine-minding, assembly-line production and automation. He concluded that those technologies which gave the worker most freedom were the least alienating. Hence, in the printing industry, which was based on craftsmanship, the worker had a large degree of freedom, whereas in the car-manufacturing industry, where workers were tied to the assembly line, there was least freedom and the workers were most alienated. According to Blauner, the technology employed in a work process is the major determinant of alienation.

Guidance notes

The first paragraph explores the origins and the meaning of the term alienation. It is always a good move to define your terms in the first paragraph. The second paragraph describes Blauner's work – note how brief this explanation is.

Criticising research methods is an easy way to pick up marks for evaluation, so you need to know methodology inside out. You can apply, this knowledge in every essay you write.

However, critics of Blauner point to a methodological flaw in his work. Blauner used questionnaires to assess the amount of alienation felt by the workers. Interactionists would argue that this is not a good way of assessing individuals' feelings and attitudes because questionnaires do not allow respondents freedom to express themselves.

This third paragraph uses the work of Goldthorpe and Lockwood as a criticism of Blauner. Goldthorpe and Lockwood's work may be old, but it is OK to use it in this essay. Firstly, because it is relevant and secondly, because the essay tracks the development of sociological research on alienation. Goldthorpe and Lockwood's work can be applied to a number of topics, e.g. work and leisure, community and voting behaviour, so it is important to know it.

Goldthorpe and Lockwood's work on *The Affluent Worker*, carried out at Vauxhall's car-assembly plant in Luton, contradicts Blaurer's findings. Goldthorpe and Lockwood found that some of the car workers had given up craft jobs which involved more freedom, in order to take car-assembly work with little freedom. The workers did this because they were 'instrumental' in their attitudes to work. This means that the workers cared little for autonomy (freedom) at work – their primary concern was for the 'amount of money' they earned. The relatively high amount of money which the workers earned at Vauxhall's enabled them to gain increased satisfaction from their life outside work. For example, they were able to buy consumer goods and take holidays away from home with their families.

However, as with Blauner's work, there are methodological problems with Goldthorpe and Lockwood's research. In particular, they have been criticised for not using a representative sample of the workforce. This means that the results of their study cannot be generalised to account for the feelings and actions of any group of workers other than those at Vauxhall's.

Support for both Blauner and Goldthorpe and Lockwood can be found in Wedderburn and Crompton's study on workers' attitudes and technology. They found that the manual workers in their study were as instrumental as those in the Vauxhall study, but also found that some of their sample's attitudes to work were influenced by technology.

This paragraph moves the emphasis from 'old' technology to 'new' technology, that is computerisation. I have also shown how technology can give more freedom to some workers, yet repress others. If you know anyone who works with computers ask them how this new technology has affected their job.

The major problem with these three studies is that they are rather outdated. More recent sociological studies have looked at the impact of computerisation upon workers' lives. Zuboff examined the effects of the introduction of information technology into a range of American companies. According to Zuboff, information technology can have two possible effects. On the one hand, it can enable an institution to become more egalitarian by allowing the workers the freedom to contribute in some way to the running of the firm; on the other hand, new technologies can be used to police workers more closely by monitoring every stage of the work process. Zuboff's investigation can be used to undermine Blauner's argument that technology is the major determinant of alienation because it shows that it is not technology in itself which is the key factor in alienation, but rather the way technology is used. In other words, new technology could be used to liberate workers or it to tighten control over them.

Just as Goldthorpe and Lockwood brought an interactionist perspective to bear on Blauner's work, so Grint and Woolgar bring an interpretivist explanation to an understanding of new technologies. Grint and Woolgar employ Foucault's notion of 'discourse' to explain the effects of computerisation. A 'discourse' is the way in which people try to make sense out of aspects of society by talking about them in a particular way. In this instance, Grint and Woolgar claim that it is the way in which the workers talk about the new technologies which affects the way they experience the technology. In other words, it is the workers' interpretation of new technologies which colours their attitudes and affects their behaviour. Therefore, it would be the workers' interpretation of the new technology and not the new technology itself which would determine alienation.

However, as Foucault would argue, it is those who have control over the discourse who have the power to determine how new technology is perceived and will consequently have the controlling definition. Grint concedes that 'experts' are more likely to have their views become the dominant ones.

Marxists would reject all the above claims whether they come from technological determinists like Blauner or interpretivists like Goldthorpe and Lockwood. According to Marxists, alienation is inevitable under capitalism no matter what technology the worker is employed on. For Marxists, it is capitalism itself which is the cause of alienation. In particular, it is the way that the capitalist organisation of work separates the workers from the fruits of their labours. Marxists see this as the explanatory factor in alienation. The capitalist class owns the means of production and the workers are forced to sell their labour to the capitalist in order to live. The capitalist owner, by virtue of ownership, is able to determine the conditions of work under the social relationships of capitalism. Not only do the workers lose the product of their labours to the capitalist owner, but they have no control over the work process. As a result, workers become alienated from work and their fellow workers. Marx believed that the same technology in a socialist society would not result in alienation because the social relationships would be different, not least in the fact that the whole of socialist society could benefit from a worker's labour rather than just the owners of the means of production.

Marx's work has, however, been heavily criticised. Some commentators have pointed to the conditions of workers in the former 'communist' countries of the eastern bloc who could be regarded as more alienated than those working in Britain (though

In the introduction, I explained that alienation is a term which was first used by Marx. This paragraph links the modern-day technology argument back to the original work of Marx to see if his ideas can still be applied. Most students, and some teachers, find Marx difficult. If you can explain Marx it will look very impressive indeed.

Where you have Marx, you are bound to have criticism. However, you can always come back with a counter-criticism or counter-explanation.

it is doubtful if Marx or Marxists would accept these countries as 'communist' or 'socialist'). Other commentators would argue that Marx's explanations of alienation are more relevant and all-encompassing than other attempts at explaining alienation. As Zuboff shows, new technology can be used in a number of ways, but is it being used in a number of ways in capitalist society?

Marxists would argue that, whatever the technology, it will be used to sustain and advance the position of the owners of the means of production. In addition, Marxists would also argue that the dominant 'discourse' concerning new technology is that it will benefit everyone in society. Most people believe this to be true and consequently will not challenge the present arrangement under capitalism.

The conclusion explores a different angle on alienation by looking at the position of house-wives. This is an issue which is very close to my heart. I hate housework and consequently I claim that I am the alienated worker both at home and at work.

In conclusion, the workplace is not the only source of alienation for many individuals. Feminists have pointed out that many women experience alienation in the home, despite technological gadgets which are meant to make life easier for the housewife. Housework could be seen as more alienating than work as it does not attract a wage, it carries no status, it can be lonely and isolating and it is monotonous. Furthermore, as feminists have pointed out, new technology has not decreased the number of hours worked by women in the home.

General comments

This essay is not the easiest in the world because it contains quite a lot of social theory. Nevertheless, a bit of effort goes a long way. Once you've got to grips with social theory, like Marxism, you can apply it to any number of essays. Remember, practice makes perfect.

Related questions

1 'Alienation is endemic to capitalism.' Discuss.

2 To what extent are automation and computerisation leading to the end of alienation?

3 'Job satisfaction is related more to pay than to any other factor.' Evaluate this statement.

Question 14

Assess the sociological argument that particular industries are prone to strikes.

Tackling the question

This is one of the questions on industrial conflict in which you will need to address the problem of the official statistics on strikes. Try to question the assertion that some industries are strike-prone. You will need to define strikes near the beginning of your essay, then you will have to produce a range of studies which explain strikes. Finally, you will need to decide, on the basis of what you have written, which, if any, of these explanations is most satisfactory to you and why. Remember that in sociology you can say almost anything as long as you back it up.

Answer

According to Hyman, a strike is a temporary stoppage of work through a collective act of paid workers in an attempt to achieve some kind of demand. An analysis of strikes shows that some types of worker, notably blue-collar workers, are more likely to be involved in strikes than other types, notably white-collar workers. This claim can be supported by looking at the statistics for strike activity in the United Kingdom which have consistently shown that assembly work and coal-mining are more likely to have strikes than other industries. However, as with many forms of 'hard' data, the statistics may not be valid measurements of strike activity. In other words, the statistics may not reflect the 'real' number of strikes that have occurred, as not all strikes are reported or recorded. Nevertheless, the miners' strike of 1984–85 does lend weight to the argument that certain industries are more strike-prone than others.

An international comparison of strikes by Kerr and Siegel found that occupations such as seamen, miners and dockers had proportionately higher strike records than other groups. They found that the factor that the 'strike-prone' workers had in common was 'community integration'. This means that the 'strike-prone' workers tended to live in occupational communities which were more or less isolated from wider society. Kerr and Siegel

Guidance notes

In this introductory paragraph I have defined what a strike is. I then go on to question the numerical evidence on strikes. You should always do this in sociology when you are presented with official statistics. I finish the paragraph with a reference to the 1984–85 miners' strike to indicate that there may be, after all, such a thing as a strike-prone industry! This questioning and re-questioning of data should earn you useful marks for evaluation.

found that this community isolation enabled a strong spirit of working-class consciousness and solidarity to grow, and acted as fertile ground for collective action such as strikes. This 'community integration' is not generally found in middle-class areas. Kerr and Siegel believe that certain industries are more prone to strikes because of the social relations which exist between community members.

I have used this paragraph to show how the 1984–85 miners' strike fits in with the arguments of Kerr and Siegel. This kind of technique will be rewarded by marks for the application of material. Later on in the paragraph I use information from the same strike to evaluate the work of Kerr and Siegel. Do remember to make sure that you use your information in a relevant sociological manner – you are not writing the history of industrial conflict in the NUM.

The example of the Yorkshire mining villages, which showed great solidarity in the 1984–85 miners' strike, can be used to support Kerr and Siegel's claim. Particularly noteworthy at this time was the formation of the support group, 'Women Against Pit Closures'. This is a further demonstration of 'community integration'. However, this strike failed. According to Scargill, this was because the TUC did not support the strike. However, others have blamed the failure on the Nottinghamshire and Derbyshire miners and their 'breakaway' rival union, the Union of Democratic Mineworkers, who were accused of 'selling out' their fellow workers. They went back to work while others were still striking. Although the miners from the Yorkshire villages had a lot of support from within their own communities, they did not receive unconditional support from mineworkers from other areas. Miners may not have the community consciousness or the solidarity which Kerr and Siegel attributed to them.

Kerr and Siegel's conclusions have also been contradicted by Hill. Hill's study of London dockworkers compared their attitudes to those held by the Vauxhall car workers in Goldthorpe and Lockwood's *The Affluent Worker*. According to Hill, London dockers' attitudes to industrial action were primarily instrumental. That is, the dockers went on strike purely for money and not for any notion of working-class solidarity.

Despite this counter-argument, the Liverpool dockers' dispute over unfair dismissal has attracted supporting strike action by dockworkers abroad, notably in Australia and North America. This demonstrates that Kerr and Siegel's argument does have some merit.

Another sociological explanation of strike-prone industries can be found in Blauner's work on alienation. According to Blauner, certain types of production technology lead to higher levels of alienation and subsequently lower levels of job satisfaction. These higher levels of alienation are likely to manifest themselves in higher levels of industrial conflict such as strike activity. One of the types of technology which, according to Blauner, produces high levels of alienation is car-assembly work such as that found at Vauxhall and Ford. It is unsurprising that sociologists have attempted to make a universal link between this type of work and strikes in their attempt to demonstrate that some industries are more strike-prone than others. Evidence shows that car manufacturing in Britain has seen a high number of strikes since the Second World War. However, the same is not true of other car-manufacturing countries such as Germany and Japan. The industrial relations record and manufacturing output of Japanese car companies have been held up as shining examples for British companies to aspire to. It appears that what may cause strikes in one country may not necessarily cause strikes in another.

Daniel and Millward's comprehensive study of strike variation found that union membership was a key factor in a strike. The more unionised a workplace, the more likely it is that the workforce will take strike action. This is supported by the work of Cronin who also found that union membership was a key factor in striking.

Ross and Hartman put forward another explanation of strike-prone industries. They compared international strike statistics between 1900 and 1950 and found that strikes were more likely to occur in work situations where there were no negotiating procedures. However, Daniel and Millward argue that strikes are more likely to occur in industries which are unionised and consequently have established negotiating procedures. Ross and Hartman were commenting on strike-prone industries as they existed between 50 and 100 years ago and their analysis of this period may be correct. Most statistical evidence, however, suggests that modern-day strikes are more likely to involve unions which have some negotiating powers.

This paragraph is an excellent example of how two separate research teams working on the same sociological phenomenon reached completely different conclusions. This is good for you because if you write about both and make them relevant, you are bound to score marks for evaluation.

Foucault's notion of discourse can be applied to explain why unionised industries are more strike-prone than others. In workplaces that are unionised it may be that the union has the power to have its explanation of the situation accepted by the workforce. The union can then persuade its members that a situation is unjust and that they should strike if necessary. In workplaces without unions, workers may be more likely to accept the management 'discourse' as there is no viable alternative.

Certainly, Hyman believes that the workers' interpretation of a situation is crucial in understanding strikes or the lack of strikes. In some industries in some cultures – the British car industry, for example – strikes may be seen as a normal and acceptable part of life. This perception of strikes would enable British car workers to take strike action more easily than Japanese car workers, who may view strikes as something to avoid at all costs. The national perception of strikes is culture-bound and must certainly play a

Using Foucault's work is another example of an application skill. Foucault is not found in the most popular A-level text, but he is well worth a read if you can find a suitable text.

part in explaining strike-proneness. The French lorry drivers' dispute of 1997 was met with shock and horror in Britain, but many other groups of French workers, including the police, were sympathetic.

In conclusion, the recent data on strikes reveal no clear and obvious pattern of strike-prone industries. Since the 1980s, successive Conservative governments have passed legislation to restrict the power of unions, and the current Labour government has stated that it will not repeal these laws. This means that even unionised workplaces will have difficulty in organising strikes. In addition, high unemployment means insecurity hangs over the heads of the majority of British workers, as there is what Marx called a 'reserve army of labour' waiting in the wings to take over their jobs. This makes strikes even less likely in the future. However, since the 1980s, strikes have occurred in some of the most unlikely industries, for example education, despite the fact that teachers tend to be more conservative than many other workers. During the 1980s and 1990s, lecturers in Further Education colleges have been forced to strike in response to restrictive new contracts. Perhaps society is about to witness different industries with a propensity to strike.

In the conclusion, I have referred to industrial conflict in further education colleges. You may have some experience of this yourself. You could put this experience to good use in your conclusion.

General comments

You need to bear in mind that strikes are not the only form of industrial conflict and there will be occasions when you will have to refer to work-related phenomena such as absenteeism and industrial sabotage.

Related questions

1   In what ways can unionisation of a workplace affect the level of industrial conflict?

2   Evaluate the importance of alienation as an explanatory factor in strikes.

3   'In modern industrial society strikes should be viewed as normal.' Discuss.

Assess the view that professional associations
are merely trade unions for the middle classes.

Tackling the question

This type of question can come up under the topics of work and stratification. The important thing for success in this question is to differentiate between upper professionals and lower professionals. This will enable you to make the argument that associations which represent upper professionals have characteristics which set them apart from lower professionals and that this means that associations that represent lower professionals are more likely to be trade unions for the middle classes.

Answer

Guidance notes

Professional associations represent occupational groups drawn from within the middle classes. The professions can be divided into two major groups – upper professionals and lower professionals. Upper professionals tend to have higher income and status, and include occupations such as doctors and dentists, whereas lower professions include occupations such as teachers and social workers. To assess the view that professional associations are merely trade unions for the middle classes, it is necessary to define a trade union. A trade union is an organisation instituted to defend and promote the interests of its members.

Functionalists such as Barber believe that higher-professional associations are more than trade unions for the middle classes. In Barber's view, higher professionals have a number of characteristics which set them apart from trade unionists. He claims that professionals like dentists have a systematic body of knowledge based on an extended period of study. Barber also argues that professionals are occupied in public service in that their work – that of doctors, for example – is in the interests of society as a whole. In addition, Barber argues that the behaviour of professionals is regulated by a code of ethics, such as the Hippocratic Oath which binds doctors.

I start off by pointing to the difference between upper professionals and lower professionals. I do not give a definition of a professional association because that is what the question is about, but I do include a precise definition of a trade union in order that professional associations can be compared with trade unions.

Note how the first sentence in this paragraph answers the question. Try to do this as often as possible in all your work. It is helpful to the examiner because it draws attention to the fact that you are trying to answer the question. In this paragraph, I'm still not defining a professional association but I am giving Barber's definition of a higher professional.

This paragraph evaluates the previous paragraph by pointing out that perhaps higher professionals are not what they claim to be. It then goes on to liken the work of professional associations to trade unions and in doing so, it directly answers the question.

This functionalist view of professionals has been criticised by both Weberian and Marxist sociologists. Taking a Weberian perspective, Parry and Parry see professionals as acting solely in their own interests. They argue that the associations which represent professionals manipulate their market position to maximise the benefits that their members receive. Professional associations do this in three ways. Firstly, they restrict the number of new entrants to the group. This leaves society with a shortage of workers in key positions. For example, there is a shortage of doctors and surgeons which is one of the causes of hospital waiting lists. However, this shortage is somewhat artificial as it is the professional associations which limit the number of entrants in the first place. This shortage of workers enables the professional associations to demand and receive high incomes. Secondly, professional associations try to maintain a monopoly in the provision of services by claiming that only their members can provide a particular service. This factor also enables professional associations to maximise the income of their members. Both these characteristics are also found in trade unions representing manual workers, like the National Graphical Association, which represented craft workers in the printing industry. Thirdly, professional associations try to put their members beyond the public eye by claiming the right to discipline them for indiscretions and malpractice. Perhaps it is only this feature which differentiates professional associations and trade unions. Nevertheless, not all professional associations have these three characteristics. As Parry and Parry point out, there is little to distinguish the professional associations which represent groups like teachers from trade unions which represent manual workers. Like many trade unions, teachers cannot control entry to the occupation. This is done by the state, and may explain the relatively low pay of teachers compared with other professions.

This is a good example of the skill of application. It uses Braverman's work on proletarianisation and applies it to teaching. This is something that you might like to discuss with your sociology tutor.

In many ways professions such as teaching have come to resemble manual work. Braverman's work on proletarianisation can be applied to explain this point. According to Braverman, many white-collar occupations have lost the advantages and privileges they held in the past. This can be illustrated by the position of teachers, particularly those employed in Further Education, who have had their salaries cut over a number of years. This cut has been achieved in two ways. Firstly, teachers have accepted wage increases less than the rate of inflation. Secondly, they have had their workloads increased. In addition, organisations have sprung up which offer to supply teaching labour (a reserve army of teaching labour) to schools and colleges at a cheaper rate, thus undermining the professional associations' ability even to protect their members' incomes. The professional associations which represent lower professionals such as teachers have been powerless to prevent these changes. This mirrors the powerlessness of trade unions representing manual workers.

Baritz, in his article 'The Servants of Power', also supports the notion that professionals are becoming proletarianised. He suggests that just as manual workers serve the interests of the capitalist class, so increasingly do professionals. Again, this can be illustrated by recent changes in the education system, which has been tied more and more tightly to the perceived needs of the capitalist economy. Even though many of these changes have been unpalatable to many teachers – the introduction of the National Curriculum, for example – the professional associations were unable to resist them. This demonstrates the lack of power and autonomy of trade unions which cannot control the destinies of their members.

An evaluation of Baritz can be found in the work of another Marxist, C. Wright Mills. Although Mills agrees with Baritz that professionals are the 'servants of the powerful' – for example, lawyers help large corporations find tax loopholes in order to maximise their profits – he claims that some of the higher professionals actually become members of the power élites through rewards such as shares and seats on the board. This group of professionals is not undergoing proletarianisation, but has experienced what Miliband would have called 'bourgeoisification'. While the professional associations which represent the lower professionals may merely be trade unions for the middle classes, the same is not true of professional associations that represent higher professionals.

Here I have introduced the work of Mills to show that some professionals become members of the bourgeoisie. This partly refutes the view that professional associations are trade unions for the middle classes.

In conclusion, the idealist and almost 'common-sense' assumptions of functionalists like Barber can only be applied to an extremely limited number of associations representing higher professionals such as judges. Most professional associations have had their status and privileges eroded by successive governments. For example, the conveyancing monopoly of solicitors has been removed, and NHS doctors and consultants have lost their autonomy and are subject to managerial directives. It is noticeable that the British Medical Association increased its membership from 70% to 80% of all doctors in 1995. However, even this increase in numbers did not mean that the BMA was able to resist unpalatable changes to the NHS, despite its threats to withdraw from participation. For academics in the Higher Education sector, work is increasingly on short-term contracts. These factors and

In the conclusion, I am using evidence to argue that some professions are in professional associations increasingly like trade unions, whereas other professionals are more like members of the capitalist class and therefore cannot be in trade unions.

others mean that organisations representing the professions are increasingly operating like trade unions in that they are forced more and more to protect the interests of their members. Some might claim that much of the change is ideological in that lower professionals do not have the same status as higher professions and have been undergoing a process of proletarianisation. There are some writers like Bennet and Hokenstadt who believe that jobs such as teaching and social work do not have and never have had the full range of professional powers, and that their workers merely aspire to be professionals. They refer to these workers as semi-professionals. Some professional groups like the National Farmers Union do not represent workers but employers. This would include groups of the self-employed, like those in the Law Society, who have no need to be like trade unions.

General comments

One useful way to prepare for this essay is to take a piece of paper, draw a line down the middle of it and then on one side write the similarities which professional associations have with trade unions, and on the other side the differences. Then see if you can incorporate all of the features into your answer.

Related questions

1 Evaluate the claim that white-collar workers are becoming indistinguishable from manual workers.

2 To what extent is it true to say that it is often difficult to differentiate trade unions and professional associations?

3 Assess the argument that although trade unions and professional associations have similar goals, the way in which they pursue these goals is completely different.

Question 16

How far is it true to say that leisure is a matter of personal choice?

Tackling the question

In the past, questions on leisure have been answered by some students using only a limited range of sociological evidence. Generally these answers have revolved around one major and quite dated study, Stanley Parker's work on leisure. The best answers to questions on leisure must refer to a wide range of studies and will almost certainly mention gender divisions.

Answer

Guidance notes

According to Parker, leisure is a period of time which is left over once other duties have been dealt with. Parker argues that a person's life can be divided into categories. Firstly, work, which Parker described as time spent working in exchange for a wage. Secondly, work obligations, which Parker cited as time taken up as a result of work but for which there is no specific pay, for example, time taken travelling to and from work. Thirdly, non-work obligations. This can include family-based tasks, like housework and childcare. Finally, time spent caring for physiological needs, such as eating and sleeping. According to Parker, leisure is the time left over once these four categories have been dealt with. The number of hours worked and the type of work a person does determine leisure. For example, consultants in a private hospital may only spend a limited amount of time working. This leaves them plenty of time to engage in leisure activities. In comparison, people working long hours in a factory may have less time to spend on leisure activities.

> In the opening paragraph, I have explained leisure using Parker's work. You could just as easily use another definition, for example, that of Elias and Dunning. It does not matter whose definition you use as long as you have a definition.

According to Parker, there are three general patterns to work and leisure: the extension pattern, where work overlaps into leisure, for example when salesmen have early morning meetings with clients on the golf course; the neutrality pattern, which is associated with low-level clerical work and factory work, where there is a definite cut-off between work and leisure, which often revolves around the family; and the opposition pattern, where

> This is Parker's argument concerning leisure. Note that it is limited to one paragraph and that the last sentence refers the question.

there is a clear break between work and leisure. Parker cites the example of mining where the workers spend long hours drinking after work. The opposition pattern is generally associated with dangerous jobs such as mining and deep-sea fishing. For Parker, the key factor which determines which leisure pattern an individual will follow is autonomy at work. Hence, Parker makes a link between the type of work an individual is engaged in and the type of leisure which that person experiences. Thus, for Parker, it is not true to say that leisure is a matter of personal choice.

However, Parker can be criticised for overlooking the effect of cultural and sub-cultural influences on leisure. For example, in Spain it is common for whole families, regardless of occupational background, to attend a bullfight. In this instance culture plays a part in determining leisure. Another criticism is that Parker's work on the opposition pattern is based on secondary data which was not collected for the purpose of the sociology of leisure and may not therefore be valid.

In this paragraph I have brought in the work of the Rapoports, I have made sure that the examiner knows that I am using it to evaluate Parker by the wording of the first sentence. Look at the wording of the first sentence and try and adopt this style. If I had just written about the Rapoports without referring to Parker, then this would almost certainly have received marks in the lower band.

According to Rapoport and Rapoport, Parker can be criticised for ignoring the influence of the family life cycle on an individual's leisure. The Rapoports argue that there are four phases in an individual's life cycle which influence that individual's leisure: (1) adolescence, during which time teenagers are looking for their personal identities. This can result in them choosing a number of leisure activities which they associate with their identity. For example, playing a variety of sports, going to concerts, experimenting with different styles of fashion and so on; (2) young adulthood where the emphasis is on individuals establishing a social identity. Leisure interests tend to become reduced during this phase, in many instances becoming centred around pursuing sexual contacts and experiences; (3) the establishment phase, where leisure becomes more home-centred with the family becoming the focal point; (4) the later years, where leisure becomes even more home-centred, for example, grandchild-centric. Thus, the age and stage of individuals in the family life cycle can determine leisure. Even though the Rapoports point to a weakness in Parker's work, they still agree that leisure is not a matter of personal choice as there are many forms of constraint on the individual. For example, someone in their forties is 'barred' from going on a Club 18–30 holiday.

Nevertheless, the Rapoports are also open to criticism. Their work overlooks the fact that age is a social construction. Society has expectations which make it difficult for individuals to pursue the leisure activity of their choice. For example, it would be very unusual to see an elderly woman at a rave, and if a middle-aged woman was dancing in a trendy club, she might be regarded by others as 'mutton dressed as lamb'. Most women would not wish to be labelled in this way, so they adapt their leisure pursuits to match their perceived stage of life. Furthermore, according to Roberts, the Rapoports based their work on case studies which are not necessarily representative of society as a whole, so the validity of their work can be called into question.

Roberts agrees that work and the life cycle can have influences on leisure, but he still believes that leisure is a matter of personal choice. He argues that if a non-work pursuit is obligatory, it cannot be leisure. For Roberts an activity only becomes leisure if someone *chooses* it as leisure. Hence, playing a round of golf in the guise of a business meeting is not leisure. Furthermore, Roberts adopts a free-market economy approach in his explanation. He claims that consumers make demands for leisure activities on organisations that provide leisure and that these organisations respond to the demands of customers. For example, clubs such as 'Cream' in Liverpool have opened in response to illegal raves. By attending illegal raves, young people gave a message to leisure organisations that there was a demand for that particular service.

> This argument by Roberts is the one on which the question is based. Poor answers will use only this study and will therefore be forced to agree that leisure is a matter of personal choice. Examiners do not want you to agree with the question.

However, Roberts does not really address the question of how that demand was created in the first place. It may be that clubs were opened as a response to raves, but the clubs now have their own culture. Young people who not old enough to get through the door of 'Cream' walk round wearing jackets and T-shirts with its logo. According to the Marxist Marcuse, the capitalist system creates false needs. Marcuse's ideas can further be applied to the relationship between work and leisure, in that work within the capitalist system does not lead to satisfaction, so workers try to find satisfaction in their leisure pursuits. However, their leisure pursuits are largely controlled by capitalism and their hard-earned money ends up back in the capitalists' pockets.

> I have introduced a Marxist analysis at this point and illustrated it with an example from club culture.

Marxists would argue that capitalism not only determines work, it also determines leisure. Even at the simplest level, the number of hours available for leisure is determined by the capitalists who set the rules on the number of hours that have to be worked. The money paid to particular occupations is also determined by capitalists, and this money, as well as time, largely determines what leisure is available. For example, there are not many Cadbury's factory workers charting yachts in Monte Carlo for the weekend. Marxists do not see leisure as a matter of personal choice.

For Clarke and Critcher, writing from a neo-Marxist position, the major factor in leisure is its commercialisation. It is now a massive capitalist business, the sole aim of which is to make profit. Large corporations attempt to manipulate consumers' desires and persuade them to buy their products. Big sportswear companies such as Reebok, Nike and Adidas have attempted to establish a hegemony (that is domination through ideas), which is so successful that even those who do not play sport feel obliged to buy and wear these makes of clothing and shoes: even the clothes that individuals wear during their leisure time is determined by capitalism. Clarke and Critcher believe that people can at best only choose their leisure from the options provided by capitalism. Consequently, leisure cannot be regarded as purely a matter of personal choice.

I have managed to bring the element of gender into the debate. Introducing gender as a factor into an answer is always likely to improve your grade, so try and do this in questions which do not appear to involve gender issues.

One of the major problems with all the theories put forward so far is that they ignore the influence of gender on leisure. There are major differences between males and females with regard to leisure. Perhaps the most important difference is that women tend to have less leisure time than men. Research by Oakley suggests that on average women spend around 70 hours a week on housework. Often women are on 24-hour call and have very little time to themselves, and so have even less choice than men over their leisure. In many cases, when young mothers do get time to themselves, they pick leisure pursuits which fit in around the children, or indeed their husbands. The idea that leisure is a matter of personal choice for many women can therefore be rejected.

In conclusion, it appears that leisure is largely shaped by an individual's occupation, position in the family life-cycle and gender. If an individual does have choice with regard to leisure, then this choice is limited and takes place within particular confines.

General comments

On occasion you may be able to apply some of the issues in your definition of leisure to answers on unemployment, because it is thought by some that as the unemployed have no work they are free to pursue leisure. Also, keep your eye on current affairs so that you are aware of the latest leisure fad. At the time of writing 'line dancing' and 'cyber pets' are two examples of fads.

Related questions

1   'Leisure reflects work.' Discuss.

2   'Work is the major determinant of leisure.' To what extent does the sociological evidence support this statement?

3   'Age is the most reliable predictor of leisure.' Evaluate this statement.

Evaluate the argument that increased patterns
of social mobility have led to a society in which
class is no longer important.

Tackling the question

Despite the length of the title, the question is asking whether social class is still important. At the time of writing there are two major studies of social mobility for England and Wales. The first is by Glass, from just after the Second World War, and the other is the 1972 Oxford Mobility Study. Thus, although one is very dated and the other quite dated you will have to use both in your answer. The examination boards know that there are only two major studies so they are looking to reward answers which show good application skills. This is an opportunity to show how you can make other sociological arguments and studies relevant to the question.

Answer

Guidance notes

When Marx was writing towards the end of the nineteenth century, he regarded social class as the vital factor which would eventually bring about the destruction of capitalism and consequently cause social change.

According to Marx, there are two major social classes in modern-day society, the bourgeoisie and the proletariat. Marx referred to these two major social classes as ideologically opposed, hostile camps. Marx predicted that, through a process of polarisation, individuals would eventually identify with either the bourgeoisie or the proletariat. Marx argued that the intermediate social classes would eventually disappear. He also predicted that the proletariat would experience immiseration, exploitation and alienation at the hands of the owners of the means of production. Marx argued that this would eventually lead to a united proletariat and the development of class consciousness, and that this class consciousness would result in the proletariat gaining the strength and the motivation to overthrow capitalism in favour of the new epoch of

In this opening section I have given the Marxist analysis of class and tied it to the question in the last sentence.

socialism. For this reason sociologists have, in the past, regarded social class as an important factor in the study of society.

In this paragraph I explain what social mobility is, as you can nearly always get marks for definitions. In addition, I have explained the different types of social mobility. Some marking schemes *insist* that the candidate give definitions and if you do not do this you will be confined to the lower mark band. You need to practise doing this.

Social mobility means movement up or down the social structure. Recent patterns of social mobility have been used in an attempt to undermine Marx's theory and the importance of social class as a measurement of society. It can be argued that there are two types of social mobility, intragenerational mobility (social mobility within a single generation), and intergenerational mobility (social mobility between different generations). Intragenerational mobility is measured by examining the occupational position of one individual at different points in that individual's life, whereas intergenerational mobility is measured by comparing and contrasting the occupational positions of sons and fathers within the same family in terms of occupational status.

At this point I state the conclusion of Glass's study as briefly as possible. The question does not ask you to write everything you know about studies of social mobility and you should avoid this kind of error.

Early work on intergenerational mobility was carried out by Glass. Glass looked at the occupational positions of a number of men and directly compared their occupations in terms of status with that of their fathers. His results showed that two-thirds of his sample had different work statuses from their fathers – a third experiencing upward social mobility and the other third downward social mobility.

Support for Glass's study of social mobility came from the Oxford Mobility Study which was carried out in 1972. The findings of this research demonstrated that in absolute terms the chances of individuals from working-class occupational backgrounds achieving a higher social class had significantly increased. This led many sociologists to comment that Britain was an open system whereby individuals could move up and down the occupational class strata, regardless of what social class they were born into. However, the Oxford Mobility Study also showed that the real chances of anyone not from a high social class achieving occupational social class 1 were limited. The study found that 45% of fathers in social class 1 had sons in social class 1, whereas only 7% of fathers in social class 7 had sons in class 1. When the results of the Oxford Mobility Study are scrutinised, it demonstrates that social class is still an important factor for measuring society.

In 1983 Goldthorpe conducted an investigation into social mobility in order to see if recession had had any impact on patterns of social mobility. Like the Oxford Mobility Study, Goldthorpe found that the levels of absolute mobility continued to rise, but in terms of relative social mobility, things had stayed static and there was no real movement between the occupational classes. According to Payne's Scottish mobility study, there were even higher rates of social mobility than Goldthorpe had found. Payne concluded that British society is more open than Goldthorpe's study shows. The advantage which Payne has over Goldthorpe is that Payne's sample includes women. It is true to say that previous sociological accounts of social mobility, which ignore the position of women, are inaccurate and cannot be used to make generalisations. It is possible that the lack of opportunities for women improves the chances of social mobility for men.

In this paragraph I play the 'gender card' to show that if we use studies of social mobility that do not include women, then the data are flawed, and we cannot drawn conclusions from them.

It is unusual for members of the proletariat to become members of the bourgeoisie and Marxists would argue that social class, as measured by the individual's relationship to the means of production, is still important to society today. However, with the collapse of 'communist' societies in Eastern Europe, Marxist analysis was thought by many to be untenable. New Right sociologists such as Saunders argue that social class is now less important in British society. According to Saunders, the major social division in British society is between home-owners who have their own transport and private health schemes, and those who do not have these advantages. In other words, the division revolves around consumerism and not social mobility.

In this section I bring in one of the New Right sociologists because he comes closest to agreeing with the proposition that social class is no longer important. It is essential that you have a range of evidence from various theoretical perspectives including the New Right. Exam boards have now started to set questions that specifically refer to the New Right.

There are self-evident truths in Saunder's argument, but it still does not explain why membership of the bourgeois class is more likely to confer the advantages he mentions than membership of the proletariat, and why it is that there is little mobility between these classes.

Whatever measure of social class is used, class-based inequalities still exist in Britain today. For example, studies of tax reforms since 1979 show how top-income earners have benefited whereas bottom-income earners have lost out. Income tax changes since 1979 have meant a redistribution of income from bottom to top. As Giddens and Scott point out, we still live in a capitalist society. This means we live in a society which is based on structured inequalities. Studies of social mobility which ignore the relationship between individuals and the means of production will continue to overlook the constant struggle between capital and labour, and will continue to find that class is no longer important.

In the conclusion, I come full circle, and go back to Marx, which is where the essay began. I conclude that if sociologists ignore the issue of ownership of the means of production, then of course class will appear to have little importance. You may not agree with this, but you should reach some kind of reasoned conclusion based on your own answer. It is much easier to write something that you believe in.

General comments

This is an example of an essay constructed on only two major pieces of research, but it is important to note that the question does not ask you to discuss social mobility in isolation. The question wants you to discuss social mobility in relation to the importance of social class. From this you should understand that you must read the question carefully, and where possible write it out in your own words. This will make it easier for you to understand its requirements.

If you know Marxist analysis well enough, you can nearly always apply it to questions in sociology. This is especially true of questions on stratification. This essay puts Marx's theory of class struggle in a nutshell. Obviously there is a lot more to Marx's theory than this. If you want to read up on Marx, do as I do and read a suitably watered-down version in the first instance.

Related questions

1   'Class is still an important factor in the life of individuals.' Discuss.

2   'Britain is a society based on meritocracy.' Explain and evaluate.

3   Examine the relationship between the social class of birth and social mobility.

Question 18

'Sociological explanations of class which ignore
gender are inadequate.' Discuss.

Tackling the question

In this instance, the question is based on a statement. In essays such as this, your task is quite simple: you must produce arguments which either support or refute the statement. If you are studying the Interboard syllabus, you will need to have an excellent understanding of stratification because it is compulsory and appears on both examination papers. Furthermore, your examination papers are weighted in favour of stratification questions. It is important to realise that gender is becoming a popular topic in A-level sociology in many areas of the syllabus, so you should make sure you know your stuff on gender and class. For this particular question you will need to cover male-dominated class analysis in order to demonstrate how important the inclusion of women is in this area.

Answer

Guidance notes

Sociological theories of social class have been criticised for largely ignoring the issue of gender in their analyses. This essay will demonstrate that gender has been ignored in a variety of social stratification studies and will argue that studies which have ignored gender are at best an incomplete and at worse an inadequate portrayal of social life.

The opening paragraph interprets the question and then goes on to say what the essay is going to do. In other words, it maps out the structure of the essay.

Early studies of social class used the male 'breadwinner' as the unit of analysis representing the family. At the time, the exclusion of women in social-class analysis was barely mentioned. This was because social class was traditionally measured by occupational position in the labour market and at that time women played a minority role in this situation. The male was seen as the head of the household, and other individuals in the same household were deemed to be of the same social class as the male breadwinner. Up until 1981, males were always seen in this position, and women living in the same household were automatically assigned the same social class as their husbands/fathers.

In this paragraph, I have put class analysis into its historical context. This helps to set the scene and demonstrates that women have been ignored in class analysis.

The first application skill is the use of the Oxford Mobility Study. As you may know, A-level sociology texts tend to explore this in enormous detail, and you must get this down to the bare minimum or you will run over on time and fail to do yourself justice in the exam.

The 1972 Oxford Mobility Study, carried out by Goldthorpe and Payne, was heavily criticised for ignoring women. They claimed that the family should be the unit of measurement, and maintained that the class position of the family was determined by the occupational position of the husband/father. Oakley argues that there are many sociological studies which use the family as a measurable unit, and that most studies take it that the unit of the family is measurable by the occupational position of the man.

Support for this method of analysis comes from Parkin who claimed that in general women have more in common with others from a similar social background, whether male or female, than they have in common with women as a whole. This means that a woman living in a small house in a council estate has more in common with her male next-door neighbour than she has with a titled woman living in a stately home. For this reason Parkin believes that the category 'women' should not be used in stratification as a unit of measurement.

I have used the work of Britten and Heath to point to the problems of using the family as a unit of measurement, citing the existence of cross-class families. This is the use of both application and evaluation skills. It is a good idea to link particular theories or studies to criticisms, as it shows that the answer has been carefully thought out.

However, according to Britten and Heath, the use of the family as a unit of measurement for stratification, based on the occupational position of the male head of household, is problematic because it does not take into account the phenomenon of cross-class families. In some situations the married couple may have occupations which belong to different layers in the social class strata. For example, a nurse, whose profession falls into social class category 2, could be married to an unskilled manual worker in social class category 7. According to early studies of social class which excluded women, the wife would be seen in this case as social class 7. Britten and Heath see Goldthorpe *et al.*'s early class analysis as flawed because the focus on the male head of household presents an untrue picture of family life. In other words, studies which ignore the existence of cross-class families can be criticised on grounds of validity. However, some sociologists still maintain that the family and the occupational position of the male head of household should be used as the unit of analysis.

More recently, Goldthorpe reiterated his commitment to the family as the unit of measurement for social-class analysis. He criticised Britten and Heath and claimed that the cross-class families of which they spoke were statistically insignificant. Nevertheless, Goldthorpe did concede that a male should not automatically be seen as the head of the household, and argued that the adult family member with the biggest commitment to the labour market should be used as the representative of the family. However, it is more common for males to hold this position of commitment to the labour market than women. One simple reason for this is that men do not have to take time out of employment to have and raise children. The occupational position of women is still largely ignored.

Britten and Heath have further criticised Goldthorpe by arguing that women's occupations do make a difference to the social class position of the family. Many women take on full-time work and are as committed to the labour market as their male counterparts. Furthermore, Britten and Heath point out that since Goldthorpe was writing there has been a dramatic rise in the number of jobs taken by women in the service industry. Many of these women have husbands who are manual workers. They argue that cross-class families are on the increase and are of increasing significance.

Further criticisms of Goldthorpe have been put forward by Stanworth who believes that men and women should be allocated to social classes according to their own individual status and not as members of a family unit. Stanworth is supported by Marshall and Rose who also believe that the unit of measurement in studies of social class should be based on the individual, which would enable the social class of women to be examined in its own right. They argue that when individuals are used as the unit of measurement, the statistics demonstrate that women have less chance of social mobility than men. If women continue to be neglected in studies, then the data obtained from studies will only present a partial picture of social class in Britain.

Some feminist writers have argued that women's social class should be analysed separately from men's. They argue that in many cases women experience discrimination in the workplace, finding it difficult to achieve high status and highly-paid jobs. The experience of women can be likened to a caste system, in which there is little social mobility, and women find it extremely difficult to work their way out of the social class they are born into. This in turn has drawn some feminist sociologists to advocate sex stratification rather than occupational stratification, as they believe that this would show more accurately how society is experienced by many women.

Studies of social class which have ignored gender have produced at best an incomplete picture of social life, and at worst an inadequate portrayal of social reality.

This penultimate paragraph introduces a different angle to the essay, that is the feminist perspective. The link between the class system and the Indian caste system is interesting. You could bring this point into other gender-based essays, e.g. gender and education. It is important to note that as yet there is not much feminist research around the topic of stratification, so keep your eyes and ears open for new information.

General comments

Knowledge about class stratification systems provides the basis for many sociology essays. I would go so far as to say that stratification is an area which can be applied to most areas on the syllabus. You could carry out your own investigation into cross-class families using the Registrar-General's Social-Class Scale, and see how many of your friends are products of cross-class families. This background knowledge will make this complex area much easier to understand.

Related questions

1 'Women are disproportionately represented in the underclass.' Discuss this statement.

2 'The increasing number of women in the job market means they can no longer be ignored in studies of social class.' Explain and evaluate.

3 How far is it true to say that women form a separate segment of the stratification system?

Question 19

'The 1990s have been characterised by
the emergence of an underclass.'
Explain and evaluate.

Tackling the question

Questions requiring knowledge of the underclass need a range of sociological material. I would suggest that you cover three perspectives, Weberian, Marxist and the New Right. Answers which rely on the Marxist and the Weberian approaches are more likely to appear in lower mark bands. Examination boards are increasingly expecting a New Right analysis. This is an essay where you might like to apply a feminist analysis by introducing the notion of the feminisation of poverty.

Answer

Guidance notes

The term 'underclass' is problematic in that there is no agreement between sociologists on what constitutes an underclass, or indeed whether an underclass exists. The term 'underclass' was originally used in Weberian analysis of social stratification. Weberians assess social class according to the status and market position of the individual, and use the term 'underclass' to describe the social group which is located at the very bottom of the social structure. This class is seen as separate from the working class. Weberians argue that an underclass is made up of people who are economically disadvantaged and consequently have a very weak market position. In addition, they believe that members of an underclass are unlikely to possess the labour skills necessary for them to be considered for employment, so demand for their services is limited. Furthermore, when employment is available, the wage that is offered is often so low that it prevents members of the underclass from participating fully in society. Weberians argue that, as a result, members of the underclass lack social status, which results in them being deemed as having very little to offer society. This results in discrimination, so the cycle of deprivation is self-perpetuating.

According to Dahrendorf, the term 'underclass' describes those who live in poverty and for whom poverty has become a way of

In this instance, I have not offered a definition of the term 'underclass'. Instead, I have told the reader that the term is problematic due to lack of agreement between sociologists. Nevertheless, I have introduced the Weberian perspective which acknowledges the existence of an underclass, and described the characteristics of those likely to be in an underclass.

life. In a similar vein, Frank Field MP defines an underclass as being made up of individuals who have little chance of escaping from poverty and a life on welfare benefits. Saunders defines an underclass as a 'stratum of people who are generally poor, unqualified and irregularly or never employed'. Saunders' New Right analysis of the underclass suggests that the underclass is on the increase, because one of his features of the underclass is deprivation, and the number of those in deprivation seems to be on the increase.

> Note that this paragraph links contemporary evidence to the notion that Britain has an underclass. Remember, to up-date this information.

Regardless of the definition of an underclass, evidence suggests that the population in this lowest stratum of society is growing. Despite government claims of all-time low numbers claiming the Job Seekers' Allowance, evidence shows that there are record numbers of claimants for other benefits which are not linked to the dole queue, for example, income support and disability and mobility benefits. In addition, there is a huge number of single mothers claiming benefits who are effectively trapped in the poverty cycle and consequently do not have the financial means to participate fully in society. The position of the poor has been exacerbated during the 1990s when there has been a redistribution of income from the lowest to the highest positions in society. The 1990s have also been a period of blame, when the poorest members of society have been seen as the 'feckless' poor and effectively blamed for their own impoverished condition.

> This paragraph introduces the issue of race to the underclass debate. Examination boards seem to like this. You should try to introduce a race or gender slant to your essays whenever you can, providing of course that it is appropriate.

Evidence put forward by Rex and Tomlinson demonstrates that members of ethnic groups are disproportionately represented within the lower echelons of society. According to Rex and Tomlinson, non-white individuals are more often found in a disadvantaged position both financially and socially. They argue that all too often members from ethnic groups do not have the material goods or benefits which are available to white members of the working class. Although they agree with the notion that the underclass is differentiated from the working class, Rex and Tomlinson perceive that members of ethnic groups fall into this category more frequently than whites. They argue that blacks are more likely to be discriminated against in education, housing and employment, and that generally they have fewer life chances than the majority of the white members of the working class. Rex and Tomlinson also argue that individuals from ethnic groups can face social discrimination in that they are often excluded from white working-class culture, and as a result are often forced to lead marginalised existences. Rex and Tomlinson describe an 'immigrant underclass', but successive government legislation has tightened immigration controls, so this part of the underclass has not increased much since the 1970s when Rex and Tomlinson first used the term. It is important to note that the number of black individuals who form part of the underclass has not gone down either.

However, we should also bear in mind that not all members of ethnic groups are found in the lowest stratum of society. Evidence demonstrates that a higher percentage of African-Asians are in the professional classes than whites.

In Weberian theory, class is marginalised while issues of discrimination and status are prioritised. However, according to Marxists, individuals from ethnic groups do not constitute a separate social class, but are objectively members of the proletariat. According to Castles and Kosack, who agree with the Weberian analysis in so far as ethnic minorities tend to be found in low-paid, low-status jobs or over-represented in the unemployment statistics, the root of the differences between black and white members of the proletariat lies in discrimination. Castles and Kosack claim that black members of the proletariat, like white members of the proletariat, often constitute a reserve army of labour. However, in terms status, it may be that the white members of this reserve army are one step of the ladder ahead of black members. Having a reserve army of labour keeps wage and pay demands down and is therefore essential for capitalism. This group of workers can be hired in times of boom and laid off in times of recession. However, Castles and Kosack believe that the proletariat is split in two. They argue that the most disadvantaged group comprises individuals from ethnic minorities, while the other group consists of indigenous whites. This is useful for the bourgeoisie because it gives them a scapegoat for Britain's housing and employment problems. This can be especially applied in the 1990s, when blacks have been scapegoated by politicians and the media for the increase in the crime rate and for the lack of housing and jobs in Britain. This can create further tension between blacks and whites and result in further discrimination. This is problematic for Marxists because while the black and white proletariat fight each other, it prevents the development of class consciousness. Marxists would reject the idea that an underclass has emerged in the 1990s but would accept that there has been an increase in the number of individuals in poverty

This section merely uses a Marxist position to evaluate the Weberian approach. If you know Marx as well as you should, it is fairly straightforward, and you could even leave out the names Castles and Kosack.

It can be argued that whether sociologists agree or disagree about the term 'underclass', there is a group in society who live below the poverty line and as a consequence are unable to participate fully in society. Although poverty in Britain is not new, the 1990s have been a period of greed and self-interest during which British

The conclusion largely states the obvious – that there is no agreement on the term underclass, so it's difficult to conclude categorically that the 1990s have been characterised by the emergence of an underclass. What do you think? Don't be afraid to draw your own conclusions; just remember to back up what you are saying.

society has become a place of 'haves' and 'have-nots', and the gap between rich and poor has grown immensely. It can be argued that people are no longer surprised to find those on benefits fitting the category of underclass. However, recent evidence on poverty shows that a quarter of all those who live in poverty in Britain today are elderly. In addition, a high percentage of those living in poverty are actually working in full-time positions. In a country where a welfare state was introduced to act as a safety net, the 1990s have seen the return of many diseases which are directly associated with poverty.

General comments

The underclass debate is more than a useful body of knowledge to possess. A lot of it can be used in essays on poverty as there are overlaps between the two subjects. You will probably have noticed that A-level sociology textbooks have sections on the underclass in their chapter on poverty. Hence, the conclusion to this question refers to the increase in poverty in the 1990s. It is possible to produce an underclass essay without referring to the Marx/Weber debate, but the exclusion of this debate will be at your peril because it is needed for the higher mark bands. It is, after all, one of the classical debates in sociology.

Related questions

1 In what way does the concept of underclass add to our understanding of poverty?

2 To what extent do you agree that the notion of an underclass is so imprecise that sociologists should ignore it?

3 Assess sociological explanations for the existence of racial discrimination in Britain.

Question 20

Evaluate the argument of some sociologists that
each society has its own culture.

Tackling the question

All sociology students will have gained some basic knowledge of culture and some might consider that this enables them to answer questions on this topic, but you cannot answer this question using a combination of basic knowledge and common sense. In order to score in the higher bands, you will need to show a range of knowledge of the terms involved in culture, and the theories surrounding culture. I would recommend that you include something on postmodernism. In addition, for this question your material must be appropriately applied to the question of whether culture is society-specific or not. Finally, evaluation of the material must be explicit.

Answer

Guidance notes

According to Linton 'the culture of any society is the way of life for its members, the collection of ideas and habits they learn, share and transmit' (Haralambos, 1995). This statement supports the notion that each society has its own shared culture. However, this essay will demonstrate that in Britain, far from a shared culture, there is a dominant culture which tends to override and dominate other cultures which also exist in Britain.

According to the functionalists Durkheim and Parsons, shared culture is an essential feature of society and the persistence of social order. Durkheim saw culture as the result of shared norms and values which are widely held by the majority of the members of that particular society.

Parsons in particular claimed that culture was transmitted from one generation to the next. The means by which this transmission occurs is the socialisation process. Throughout an individual's lifetime, the individual learns the culture of the society into which he or she was born (assuming that the individual stays within that society). Some examples of agencies which transmit

This is a straightforward opening in that it offers a definition of the term culture, and then it proceeds to say what arguments the essay will contain.

This is a fairly simple statement of the functionalist position which you can find in the first chapter of many A-level sociology texts. In a number of schools and colleges, you will cover this in your introduction to sociology, possibly in induction weeks. This is an example of applying material from a different place in the syllabus.

Here I start to write about different sorts of culture. I could have used folk culture, mass culture or working-class culture. Perhaps you might include these terms in your answers.

I think that this is a really important part of the essay. This mention of postmodernism is fairly brief but it is the kind of argument that examiners are looking for. If you can put it in your answers, it can move you higher up the mark band.

Gilroy is one of the writers at the Centre for Contemporary Cultural Studies, and you may have come across him in your study of neo-Marxists on deviance. If you use this work make sure you read

culture are the family, the education system, the workplace, the peer group and the mass media. Anyone who rejects the main-stream culture of that society or has not internalised the culture may be perceived as deviant. For example, travellers are frequently seen as deviant and their behaviour is punishable under the Criminal Justice and Public Order Act 1994. This would suggest that the majority of individuals in each society have their own shared culture.

However, while it could be argued that within the culture of British society there are many competing cultures, the prevailing ideology is loaded with values and judgements which mean that one culture is regarded as being worth more than any other. The dominant culture is the one to be aspired to. Some sociologists use the term élite culture to refer to certain forms of the dominant culture, such as the everyday culture of the higher social classes, like smoking Monte Cristo cigars, and being a member of gentlemen's clubs. This kind of culture is the exclusive domain of the wealthy. Another form of culture is mass culture which tends to refer to the culture enjoyed by the rest of society. By contrast, high culture, which also has the notion of superiority within it, refers to certain kinds of music, literature and art. These, however, are not exclusive to the well-off.

More recently, the term 'popular culture' has been used instead of mass culture, because the term mass culture was seen to be so value-laden. Postmodernists tend to reject the differences between high culture and popular culture. Writers such as Strinati have claimed that popular culture has increasingly taken over other forms of culture. This is due to the advances within mass communication, such as television, which can bring culture into living-rooms. The previously narrow-banded culture of opera, for example, has been brought to the mass of the population via television and compact discs. The large number of individuals who watched the televised concerts of Pavarotti and who buy his compact discs lend empirical support to this claim. This postmodernist argument supports the notion that society has its own shared culture.

However, élite culture is an aspect of the dominant culture to which the majority of the population has no access owing to birth or lack of finance. Unlike other subcultures, élite cultures are not viewed as deviant. Gilroy points out how British culture has had difficulty in accepting black culture. He was writing about Caribbean culture, but a more recent example of an alternative and vibrant subculture in Britain is Islam. Followers of Islam have their own particular design for living which is seen by many as a threat to the established British subculture. Politicians such as Norman Tebbit refuse to accept that Britain is a multicultural society and claim that British society has its own shared culture, but this assertion does not stand up to close scrutiny.

The Marxist proposition that the ideas of the ruling class are the ruling ideas of any epoch can be applied to explain why each individual society believes that all members of that particular society share a culture. According to Marx, the dominant ideology of any society will reflect and protect the interests of the ruling class. In contrast with functionalist analysis, Marxists claim that the culture which is transmitted from one generation to the next generation is a form of brainwashing by which the subject class, namely the proletariat, accept the ideas of the dominant class, namely the bourgeoisie. A major part of the culture is the idea that there is one culture which is shared and therefore that alternative cultures are deviant and threatening to British culture in some way. Even when a culture is not shared and is initially perceived as a threat, it can eventually be absorbed into capitalism. In his work, *Subculture: the meaning of style*, Hebdige looks at the rise of punks with their anti-establishment attitudes and anti-fashion appearance of plastic bin-bags, razor-blades and safety-pins. This style could be seen as resistance to the capitalist ideology of rampant consumerism, but it was not long before the fashion industry was selling designer ripped clothes to up-and-coming punks. Similarly, it is interesting to note how illegal raves have become a multi-million pound industry. As Marx wrote, the ideas of the ruling class are in every epoch the ruling ideas. Why should the ideas governing culture be any different?

up on the Italian Marxist Gramsci because the CCCS base a lot of their work on Gramsci.

The notion that culture comes mainly from the capitalist class can be found in the work of the Frankfurt School. They claimed that the capitalist class, through its ownership of the mass media, is able to manipulate the tastes, wants and needs of the proletariat. This notion is not as far-fetched as it sounds. Using the example of the widespread adoption of the football shirt as a form of dress, it can be suggested that capitalists have persuaded large numbers of the proletariat to pay an inflated amount of money for a cheap polyester garment, and for the privilege of displaying three or more advertisements for capitalist products. These products include the football club, the sponsor, the player (who is also a product), and the maker of the shirt. To conclude, the proletariat act as culture bearers, not for their specific society, but for the values of international capitalism.

At the end of the answer I merely restate my conclusion which I started with in the opening paragraph, but I also use application skills by illustrating it through the marketing of football shirts – you can buy wallpaper and other accessories in your favourite team strip!

General comments

Culture is a new area on the sociology syllabus, and consequently there is very little in the way of information on culture in the most popular A-level sociology textbooks. If you choose to prepare this topic, you need to keep up to date by reading periodicals such as *Sociology Review*. Students with a particular interest in youth subcultures may well prefer to apply this material to the question. In this case you might like to apply material from delinquency subculture which you should have covered in the sociology of deviance. This would show additional application skills.

Related questions

1   Discuss the proposition that society determines culture.

2   'In recent years there has been a tendency for popular culture to absorb higher forms of culture.' Assess this statement.

3   To what extent does culture differ from ideology?

Question 21

Assess sociological contributions to our understanding of delinquency.

Tackling the question

This question is asking for a critical assessment of sociological explanations of delinquency. Its wording should tell you that sociological accounts of delinquency are problematic and therefore easy to criticise. In general, crime and deviance essays are popular among students. This means that if you choose to answer the crime and deviance section in the examination, you will have a lot of competition, so you must learn to make your essays strong and concise. You also need to make sure that you link your answer to the question.

Answer

One of the major sociological contributions to our understanding of delinquency can be found in Cohen's work, *Delinquent Boys*. For Cohen, delinquency is a collective and frequently non-utilitarian deviant act found among lower-working-class boys. According to Cohen, all boys aspire to the middle-class value of success, such as is achieved through educational qualifications. However, the evidence suggests that it is middle-class boys and 'respectable' working-class boys who mainly achieve educational success. In comparison, boys from the lower working class more often than not under-achieve in education. Cohen argues that lower-working-class boys are unable to compete in the education system because they are culturally deprived. This results in 'status frustration' for them. One way in which they solve this problem of 'status frustration' is to react collectively by turning middle-class values upside down, and awarding status for acts which oppose middle-class culture. In other words, this delinquent subculture reverses society's norms and values. Within the delinquent subculture, status is achieved through behaviour such as fighting, vandalism, truanting and drug-taking, in other words through general anti-social behaviour. Hence for Cohen, delinquency is the result of a reaction to lack of status in society.

Guidance notes

The essay launches straight in with Cohen's work on delinquency subculture. It offers a detailed but short explanation of his contribution to the understanding of delinquency. You could spend longer on Cohen but this would be at the cost of other material and would limit your range of contributions, thereby jeopardising your chance of achieving a higher mark band.

In this second paragraph I have used of the work of Hargreaves to support Cohen. Again, note how concise this paragraph is. It would be easy to write reams about triple failures but this would not attract any more marks.

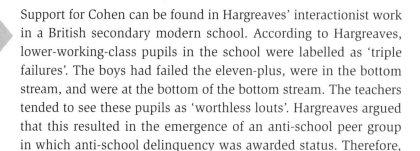

Support for Cohen can be found in Hargreaves' interactionist work in a British secondary modern school. According to Hargreaves, lower-working-class pupils in the school were labelled as 'triple failures'. The boys had failed the eleven-plus, were in the bottom stream, and were at the bottom of the bottom stream. The teachers tended to see these pupils as 'worthless louts'. Hargreaves argued that this resulted in the emergence of an anti-school peer group in which anti-school delinquency was awarded status. Therefore, for Hargreaves, delinquency is the result of negative labelling.

However, Box disagrees with Cohen. He claims that lower-working-class boys do not have the same middle-class values as the school, but the way they are seen as failures leads to resentment. For Box, this resentment can result in the lower-working-class boys turning against authority, and consequently forming delinquent subcultures.

The essay now moves away from supporting evidence to critical evidence. Remember that exam papers are weighted so that you can score higher marks for demonstrating evaluation skills.

Miller also criticises Cohen's argument that delinquency is caused by 'status frustration'. For Miller, delinquency is the result of the different and distinctive culture of the lower working class. According to Miller, lower-working-class life is characterised by a set of 'focal concerns', that is areas of interest and involvement which consist of: being in trouble rather than out of it; being tough and masculine; being smart and street-wise; enjoying exciting activities; being free; and having a fatalistic attitude, which manifests itself in a belief in luck or chance – if you get caught, that's just the way it goes. Miller claims that these focal concerns are likely to lead lower-working-class boys into trouble with the authorities. The values within this subculture are exaggerated because of status insecurity.

Bordua claims that for Miller's portrayal of lower-working-class life to be accurate, the whole class must be cut off and isolated from the rest of society, and social agencies and institutions have no impact on it. It may be that Bordua seriously underestimates the diversity of values, beliefs, and life styles in today's multicultural society. In addition, it is difficult to demonstrate that lower-working-class boys either accept or reject middle-class success goals. Two British studies, *Learning to Labour* by Willis, and *Schooling the Smash Street Kids* by Corrigan, seem to suggest that they do not share middle-class goals and values in the first place.

Willis does not accept Cohen's theory of delinquency. His study, which combines interactionism and Marxism, shows that the lower-working-class boys are already aware of their comparative failure. In addition, they are not looking for success along middle-class lines. This rejection of middle-class norms and values results in a subculture which is in opposition to the culture of the school. The boys do not attend school in order to achieve, but rather they go to school to have a 'laff' (laugh). This behaviour which is at odds with the school is perceived as delinquent, but may in fact be a natural response to the boys' position in the class structure.

In a similar way, Corrigan shows that football hooliganism as a form of delinquency can be a response by young lower-working-class males to the alienation of both school and dead-end working-class jobs. Football hooliganism is a form of behaviour which enables them to do something worthwhile, in that they can achieve status from their actions. Football hooliganism is similar to truanting and other deviant behaviour in that it gains respect from other boys. However, Corrigan can be criticised. Evidence suggests that football hooliganism is not just a lower-working-class pastime. Recently evidence from television documentaries has demonstrated that in some cases football hooliganism is highly organised and involves males with 'respectable' middle-class jobs in the City. Furthermore, it is doubtful whether many lower-working-class youths can afford to travel abroad to watch football matches and participate in football hooliganism in foreign countries.

In this paragraph, I have used Corrigan's work on football hooliganism to support the subcultural approach to delinquency. However, the same paragraph also criticises Cohen. Note how I have used Corrigan's own example of football hooliganism to evaluate his work. I don't know much about football, but logic dictates that the average lower-working-class boy can't afford to travel across the world to watch a game of soccer.

Matza argues that these theories of delinquency subculture tend to present delinquency as a widespread, collective, lower-working-class activity, whereas in reality many delinquent acts are committed by individual youths and not necessarily by groups of lower-working-class youths. Matza also argues that lower-working-class youths do not regularly take part in delinquent activity, rather they drift in and out of delinquent ventures. Therefore, unlike some of the other theories concerned with juvenile delinquency, Matza sees delinquency as a voluntary activity and not a way of life which is caused by social forces or subcultural norms.

All of the theories and writers that have been discussed can be criticised for ignoring middle-class delinquency and female delinquency. Chambliss shows how similar delinquent behaviour within groups of working-class youths and middle-class youths is interpreted differently by the agencies of social control. Chambliss compared the criminal activities of a group of working-class youths, whom he called the 'roughnecks', and the criminal activities of a group of middle-class youths, whom he referred to as the 'saints'. Chambliss was interested in the way their behaviour was seen and consequently labelled by the police. Chambliss found that despite the fact that the 'saints' engaged in more

Chambliss' work on crime can be applied to a number of crime and deviance essays, so make sure you know about the 'roughnecks' and the 'saints'.

delinquent behaviour than the 'roughnecks', the 'roughnecks' attracted more attention from the agencies of social control. Meanwhile the 'saints' did not get as much as a parking ticket between them. Chambliss can be supported by applying Becker's work. Becker claims that if a fight occurs in a working-class area, the police are more likely to label this as a show of delinquency. However, if a fight occurs in a middle-class area, the police are more likely to see this as a demonstration of 'high spirits'.

The final paragraph comments on the lack of explanations for female delinquency. Again this is a criticism which can be used in a number of crime and deviance essays. Don't worry if you make the same evaluation point in a number of essays. Some examples just have more uses than others.

Finally, all the above material can be criticised for ignoring female delinquency. It can be argued that if Cohen is correct, then just as much criminality should be seen amongst lower-working-class girls. Recent studies on female crime by sociologists such as Campbell, suggest that there has been a rise in female delinquency. However, as Smart argues, while sociology and criminology are dominated by men and are about the study of men, much female crime will continue to go uncovered.

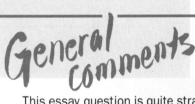

General comments

This essay question is quite straightforward. The only problem is that there is so much information available that you will have to choose what to include and what to exclude. This is not the easiest thing to do when you are under pressure, so you need to practise this skill. Crime and deviance is arguably one of the most interesting areas on the sociology syllabus. It is also one of the most popular. This means that some students know more about crime and deviance than other topics. Do not let this lead you into spending more time on crime and deviance at the expense of other topics in the examination. You really need to spend an equal amount of time on each essay in order to achieve the higher grades.

Related questions

1 'Crime is mainly a working-class, male and urban phenomenon.' Discuss.

2 Why do delinquent subcultures develop?

3 How have functionalist theories of crime and deviance explained youth crime?

'The continuing myth of black criminality is undeserved.' Discuss.

Tackling the question

The relationship between race and crime has become quite popular for some examination boards. The very wording of this question implies that black criminality is a myth. In this essay you will be expected to show how, and why, black people are over-represented in the crime statistics. You will also be expected to write knowledgeably about discrimination and stereotyping, and the role of the police in creating this stereotypical image of the black criminal.

Answer

Guidance notes

The official statistics shows that in relation to 'street crime', such as assault, robbery and drug-selling, young Afro-Caribbeans are over-represented in the official crime statistics. This has led many individuals, certain governments and the mass media to view members of ethnic minorities as having a higher propensity to commit crime than white individuals. However, the latest Home Office research demonstrates that there is very little difference between blacks and whites in their propensity to commit crime. Furthermore, the Home Office research suggests that whites are more likely to be involved in drug-related crime than blacks. There are a number of arguments which attempt to explain why black criminality seems disproportionately high.

The paragraph sets the scene in that it looks at and questions the official statistics. When you are presented with any form of official statistics you should always try to question their reliability and validity.

Interactionists would claim that the police hold stereotypical notions of who is more likely to commit crime. This is a point taken up in Gilroy's neo-Marxist analysis of black criminality. He claims that the high concentration of blacks in the official crime statistics is the result of the racist policies of the police. According to Gilroy, the police are more likely to stop and arrest blacks because they perceive blacks to be heavily involved in 'street crime'. Therefore, police practices mean that more blacks will end

The essay quickly launches into the interactionist position on crime and deviance by linking stereotyping to the high crime statistics for blacks. I then apply the work of Gilroy who explores the racist policies of the police. You should note that there are

two main aspects to Gilroy's work
and that this paragraph only
covers one of them. You may be
able to find some specific
examples to support Gilroy.

up as an official statistic, not because they are more criminal than
whites but because of police activity.

This aspect of Gilroy's work is supported by Holdaway's
participant observation study of the police force. Holdaway
claimed that there was a 'culture of policing', by which he meant
that some police officers hold stereotypical and prejudiced percep-
tions of who are the 'typical' criminals. This fact, coupled with
police discretion, meant that some groups, especially blacks,
would be more likely to appear in the official statistics.
Furthermore, as Pilkington points out, the police have a considerable amount of discretion in recording crime, which may mean
that black crime is more likely to be recorded.

Lea and Young claim that police racism cannot totally explain
the number of blacks in the official statistics, because the majority
of crimes are brought to the police's attention by the public and
are not discovered by the police. However, according to Holdaway,
the police have discretion in determining firstly, whether an arrest
is made, secondly, what the charge should be, and thirdly, whether
a caution is issued. Therefore, the police play a role in deciding
whether a reported crime actually becomes recorded.

In this paragraph I have used the
example of increased policing
in Brixton to support Gilroy.
Remember, if you use examples
to demonstrate your point, try to
be as concise as possible.

Further support for this part of Gilroy's work comes from Kettle's
work on 'Operation Swamp'. This shows how increased policing
in Brixton, a black area in London, doubled the number of arrests.
On face value it would seem that black criminality had increased.
However, in reality the increased arrests were a result of increased
policing, and the same results would probably have occurred if
heavy-handed policing tactics had been carried out in a white
area. The 1981 Brixton riots followed 'Operation Swamp' and led
to a further 'increase' in black criminality. It could also be argued
that the death of Wayne Douglas in December 1995 whilst in police
custody sparked off riots which affected the crime statistics for
Brixton in that year. These last pieces of evidence suggest that
'black criminality' is partly caused by police action. It could be
argued that if the police treated black people in the same way as
white people, and policed black areas in the same way in which
they police white areas, then the crime statistics for blacks might
be considerably lower. Unfortunately, the 1997 survey into police
attitudes reveals that the majority of police still hold racist
attitudes, and this is likely to manifest itself in police work. Until
the police act in an even-handed way towards blacks and whites,
there is no real way of measuring the validity of black criminality.

The second aspect of Gilroy's
work is now covered. It links black
crime to conscious political acts.

Another aspect of Gilroy's work seems to argue that black criminality is not necessarily a myth. Following the work of Taylor,
Walton and Young, Gilroy claims that black criminals choose to

break the law. In other words, black crimes are often conscious and sometimes deliberate political acts. Gilroy believes that as the descendants of immigrants to Britain, blacks have a historical legacy of organised struggle against exploitation. This means that blacks are, to some extent, politically organised, and the demonstrations and riots which have occurred in black inner-city areas are evidence of this political struggle. Thus, on the one hand, Gilroy offers an explanation as to why black individuals are over-represented in the statistics for 'street crime', and on the other hand, an explanation for collective crimes such as riots.

Hall *et al.* do not believe that most deviance is political. They argue that 'street crime' tends to involve individuals stealing from their own kind. This hardly makes stealing a political act. Nevertheless, they attempt to show how the 'epidemic' which came to be known as 'mugging' and occurred at the beginning of the 1970s, was the result of a number of problems faced by British capitalism at that particular time. Although there is no crime called 'mugging', during this period newspapers used the term to describe a range of street crimes. The national press reported these crimes as if they were new, which they were not; they merely had a different label attached to them. The result of this over-reporting was a moral panic about street crime. The main perpetrator of this 'new phenomenon' was seen to be young, male, urban and black. According to Hall *et al.*, the 'black mugger' provided a useful scapegoat who diverted the public's attention away from the crisis within British capitalism. From the Second World War until the early 1970s there had been a reasonable amount of economic prosperity for the majority of the population, but in the early 1970s living standards failed to rise, and increasing unemployment became a threat. Young blacks were scapegoated for white unemployment and the increase in crime, so the public were led to be critical of blacks rather than the capitalist system. Hall *et al.* point to the important role of the mass media in this scapegoating process. They do not mean that the mass media conspired against the black population, nor that the media were manipulated by the government, but that only 'experts' such as the police and politicians have access to the media and therefore the picture given by the mass media is narrow. This means that media reporting of 'mugging' is partly responsible for the myth of black criminality.

At this point the essay becomes quite complex because it links the scapegoating of blacks to a crisis in the capitalist system. I have used examples such as high unemployment to demonstrate the crisis. Keep your eye on the unemployment statistics because up-to-date information always looks impressive. I have taken care to spell out that this scapegoating is not the result of a conspiracy. Some students with a poor understanding of Marxism seem to think that everything in society is a capitalist conspiracy. This kind of weak understanding does not impress examiners. The mechanisms of capitalism are much more sophisticated than conspiracy.

Hall *et al.* also seem to accept the notion of black criminality. They claim that the economic crisis of the 1970s hit Afro-Caribbeans more than whites. The unemployment rate for blacks was, and still is, far higher than that for whites. This was

In this paragraph I mention both Hall and Pryce who accept the notion of black criminality. The essay has taken two angles, firstly, that black people are not as criminal as the statistics make out, and secondly, that when black people do commit crime it is the result of other factors influencing their behaviour, e.g. politics and poverty.

especially the case among school-leavers. In addition, the only type of work available for young blacks tended to be menial, low paid and low status. According to Hall *et al.*, blacks then turned to 'hustling' to make a living. 'Hustling' includes street crime, drugs and prostitution. Pryce's participant observation study in Bristol lends support to Hall *et al*. He claimed that 'hustlers' originally wanted decent work with good wages but could only find 'white man's shit work' and therefore turned to selling drugs, pimping and conning. It is important to note that Pryce's study also showed that the majority of West Indians were law-abiding church attenders. Nevertheless, this aspect of Afro-Caribbean culture receives little attention from the mass media.

One of the major problems with Hall *et al.*'s work is that they want to have it both ways. On the one hand they are saying that black criminality is made worse by police labelling, and on the other hand they are saying that black criminality is inevitable given the rate of black unemployment in Britain.

In conclusion, it appears that problems with the validity and reliability of the official statistics mean that the debate concerning black criminality cannot be resolved. And until there is real equality between blacks and whites in British society, the criminal propensity of either group cannot be fully examined.

General comments

Knowledge of race and criminality provides a basis for several other topics in the sociology of deviance. The information can be applied to essays on crime statistics and on labelling theory. The Hall research can also be used in essays on the mass media and on politics. The neo-Marxist approach is quite academically demanding: you need to read around the Hall research in order to develop a better understanding of it.

Related questions

1   Evaluate the argument that immigration has led to increased crime levels.

2   'Black people are over-represented in the crime statistics.' Discuss.

3   'The emphasis on black crime has meant that society has overlooked major social problems.' Assess this statement.

Examine the strengths and weaknesses of an
interactionist approach to deviance.

Tackling the question

The interactionist approach to deviance is an extremely popular topic for A-level sociology students. In this case, the question demands that the strengths and weaknesses of interactionism are examined. In other essays it is possible to achieve a numerical balance between the strengths and weaknesses of an approach. However, in this instance, a numerical balance is quite difficult to achieve, because interactionism is such a major departure from functionalist theories of deviance, in that it shows that it is important to look at what happens to deviants after they have been found out. This was the only sociological theory at the time which did this, and as a consequence is largely beyond reproach in this respect. The fact that a balance is hard to achieve in this instance is recognised by examiners who tend to look for evaluation points which commend the strong aspects of the interactionist theory of deviance.

Answer

Guidance notes

The functionalist perspective on deviance focuses on the biographical details of the deviant, such as what motivates the deviant to act in a particular way, and/or what social forces and pressures govern the actions of the deviant. In comparison, the interactionist approach to deviance looks at how and why individuals and groups are seen as deviant, and examines the relationship between those who are labelled as deviant and those who are able to define an act as deviant, for example, the relationship between the pupil and the teacher, or between the police officer and the criminal.

In the opening paragraph, I have briefly compared the functionalist approach to deviance with that of interactionism. This clearly spells out the difference between the two perspectives. There is no need to expand on the functionalist perspective. That is not what the essay is asking you to do.

According to Becker, writing from an interactionist perspective, certain groups in society have the power to make the rules and determine what constitutes deviance. For Becker an act cannot be *classified* as deviant until it has been *labelled* as deviant. Some groups in society have the power to create a label and to make that label stick – for example, a teacher can label pupils as deviant because they have been disruptive in class. Through a series of

This paragraph offers an explanation of labelling. Note that I use an example to illustrate the point, in this instance the example of a teacher labelling a pupil. Most students can identify with this. I expect that most of you can think of a time when a teacher has done this, either positively or negatively.

measures, such as sending letters home, writing reports about those particular pupils, and discussion with other members of staff, a teacher can give pupils a negative label that can affect them for the rest of their lives.

However, Becker claimed that it is the circumstances which surround a particular act which determine whether or not the act is seen as deviant: it depends on who commits the act, when the act is committed, where it is committed and who sees it. For example, spectators running onto a football pitch at the end of the match are seen as deviant, whereas spectators running onto a rugby union pitch are not perceived in the same way. In addition, deviance has a historical aspect to it. For example, in Britain up until the 1870s it was usual for men to bathe naked at the beach, but by 1872 it was considered improper, and men had to wear drawers, which also came to be seen as immodest and were replaced by bathing costumes covering most of the arms and legs. The strength of interactionist theory is that it shows the importance of society in creating deviance. In other words, unlike in previous functionalist theories, society, not the deviant, is seen as responsible for deviance.

In this paragraph I have explained the consequence of deviance.

Another strength of interactionism is that it points to the effects of being labelled a deviant. According to Becker, labels are not neutral. They designate an individual as a particular sort of person. In other words, a label is an evaluation of an individual. A label can become an individual's 'master status'. This is a label which over-rides all other labels. An example is that a man might be a father, husband and brother, but 'paedophile' over-rides these labels. Becker argues that the master status can become part of a person's self-image which may result in the deviants seeking out others like themselves, until eventually the label produces a self-fulfilling prophecy. For example, pupils who have been labelled as troublemakers, thrown out of classes, and possibly excluded from school, may take up the label of troublemakers. They may start to live up to the label. Hence, the label 'troublemakers' becomes their master status and can become a self-fulfilling prophecy. Furthermore, they may seek out other troublemakers and truants from school and get involved in additional deviant acts, such as shoplifting.

This paragraph focuses on support for Becker's work with an example of an interactionist study which was carried out in Liverpool. As I live in Merseyside, I tend to use a lot of examples

This element of Becker's argument can be seen in Gill's work, *Luke Street*. This is an interactionist study of a 'tough' area of Liverpool. Gill claims that employers saw 'Luke Street' as a bad neighbourhood and were reluctant to employ anyone with a Luke Street address. In addition, Gill argues that men from Luke Street felt obliged to fight simply because they were expected to be 'hard' and had to live up to the expectation of being 'tough'. The inter-actionist approach to deviance is stronger than positivism, because it looks at the effects of criminalisation on the individual.

This strength is clearly demonstrated in Young's study of 'hippy' marijuana smokers. Young looked at the meanings which the police put on the hippies and their behaviour as a conse-quence of this label. The police perceived the hippies as dirty, lazy, scruffy, drug-smoking individuals. Young claims that as a result, the hippies withdrew into themselves and excluded all outsiders, and that marijuana-smoking became a central life concern. He also suggests that the hippies went on to exaggerate the difference between themselves and wider society by growing their hair even longer and wearing even more outlandish clothes. It would seem that police reaction to deviant behaviour 'caused' the deviance to escalate.

Lemert takes labelling theory a stage further by emphasising the importance of societal reaction. He distinguishes between primary deviation and secondary deviation. Primary deviation is deviance which has not been labelled. For example, most people steal something at least once in their life, but they are not perceived as deviant until they are caught stealing. Secondary deviation consists of the response of the individual to societal reaction to the deviant act, so in this case it would be how the deviant acts as a result of the reaction to the theft.

which relate to the area. You might like to see if any famous studies have been carried out in a locality near you. It helps to make the issue under investigation more relevant to you personally.

Another interactionist, Cicourel, looked at the delinquency rates in two similar Californian cities. If positivist theories of deviance are accurate, both cities should have similar rates of delinquency, because according to this approach social forces are the cause of deviance, and the social forces would be the same for both cities. However, Cicourel found a significant difference in the delin-quency rate for the two cities. One city employed more juvenile officers than the other city. Consequently, this city had a higher delinquency rate. In the other city the delinquency rate went up and down according to police activity, which itself was determined by pressure from outside agencies such as the local newspaper or the Mayor. Cicourel's study clearly demonstrates the importance of societal reaction.

In addition, Cicourel studied the process by which offenders became labelled as deviants. According to Cicourel, justice is subject to negotiation, that is, the interaction which takes place between the offender and the agencies of social control. He found that the police have a stereotypical picture of what constitutes a 'typical delinquent'. This image is based on the appearance, language, accent, and social class of the offender. It could be argued that the police do not have unlimited budgets and prisons do not have unlimited spaces, so agencies of social control are

Cicourel provides a useful example of an interactionist study, as it not only explains the importance of societal reaction, but also how stereotyping can lead to labelling. Cicourel's work can be used in other essays, in particular essays on crime statistics.

forced to be selective. On the other hand, this does not make it right. Cicourel found that middle-class offenders were more likely to be let off with a caution, whereas working-class offenders were more likely to be arrested and charged. Again, a strength in the interactionist approach to deviance as used by Cicourel is that it uncovers relationships which would go undetected in other methods of investigation.

This paragraph looks at the two major weaknesses of the interactionist approach to deviance. All in all, it is difficult to criticise the interactionist approach because of the unique contribution it makes to our understanding of deviance. You could make individual criticisms about each interactionist's work as you go through the essay, but these would not necessarily detract from the strengths of the theory.

There are two major weaknesses in the interactionist approach to deviance. Firstly, interactionism offers no explanation for primary deviation, that is why individuals commit a deviant act in the first place. Bank robbers do not become bank robbers because someone has labelled them as bank robbers. Secondly, interactionists fail to explore the relationship between deviance and power. Why is it that some have the power to label, and others do not? It is easy for teachers to label a pupil as a troublemaker, for example, but difficult for a pupil to label a teacher as inadequate.

The interactionist study of deviance can also be criticised for making the assumption that nothing is deviant until it has been labelled as such. It can be argued that some things, such as murder or rape, are always wrong.

In the concluding paragraph I have summarised the strengths of the interactionist approach to deviance. In addition, I also advocate a combination of approaches. This is known as methodological pluralism and it shows the examiner that you have a good awareness of which approaches could work together.

In conclusion, the interactionist study of deviance has obvious strengths: it takes a new approach to deviance and uncovers attitudes held by law-enforcement agencies. It also explores the results of labelling on the individual, while not regarding the offender as abnormal. It may be that the study of deviance requires a synthesis of approaches in order that the strengths of one approach may counteract the weaknesses in another, and vice versa. One possible combination would be to use interactionism alongside Marxism for a fuller understanding of deviant activity.

General comments

If a question like this appears on the examination paper, it is bound to be very popular, so make sure that your knowledge and understanding of the material are first-rate. When examiners are faced with a large number of responses on a popular question, they are really pleased to find one which has been well-written. In order to achieve a sufficient level of understanding on this topic, you must read a number of A-level texts. Do not rely on your lesson notes or any one text. Many students believe that labelling theory has more validity than other theories because they themselves have been labelled. Even so, it is absolutely critical to make sufficient evaluations in order to achieve the highest grade possible.

Related questions

1 How far is it true to say that both the nature and the extent of deviance are socially constructed?

2 'Deviance is in the eye of the beholder.' Discuss.

3 Assess the argument that the police have the power to choose who and what is deviant.

Question 24

'Women continue to be under-represented in the crime statistics because the agencies of control are less likely to see women as criminals.' Evaluate this statement.

Tackling the question

Female criminology is an issue which has been neglected for many years by sociologists and criminologists. It is only recently that female-crime studies have found their way into A-level sociology textbooks. The essay title itself uses the term 'under-represented' to describe the position of women in the official crime statistics. This indicates that the essay requires an exploration of the official crime statistics in the first instance. The question points to the possibility of a relationship between this under-represented figure and the agencies of social control. Thus, you will have to provide an explanation of what agencies of social control actually are and their role in creating statistics. You will then have to explore the evidence which supports or refutes this relationship, and present alternative explanations.

Answer

I begin by describing the typical offender according to the crime statistics and have used a Home Office report to contradict them. I question the reliability of the official crime statistics from the start.

Pollak was writing in the 1950s, but his work is still important for this essay because he introduced the 'chivalry thesis'. His claims about women poisoning their relatives, sexually abusing their children, hiding their period pain and faking orgasms make Pollak a hard man to forget.

According to the official statistics, crime is a predominantly male, working-class phenomenon. However, a Home Office report shows that the gap between the sexes is not as wide as the statistics indicate. This essay will explore why females tend not to become crime statistics even though they commit crimes.

The early work of Pollak claims that the official crime statistics for women are highly misleading and hide the true extent of female crime, much of which, he says, goes unreported. Pollak suggested that women's domestic role of housewife/mother gave them the opportunity to hide crimes such as poisoning their relatives, and sexually abusing their children. He also argued that women are naturally devious and as a result are more adept at concealing their crimes. Pollak attributed this to biology. As proof of their inherent dishonesty, he cited their concealment of menstrual pain both from men and from society, as well as their ability to fake orgasms. In addition, Pollak argued that the police, magistrates, courts and judges are more likely to be lenient towards women once their crimes have been reported. Pollak referred to this as the 'chivalry thesis'. This suggests that because women are seen as subordinate, caring and weak they are thought to be incapable of malicious crime. According to this position, the reason female crime is under-represented in the official crime statistics is the inbuilt sexism in the legal process.

Although Pollak can be criticised for being biologically deterministic and sexist in his own attitudes and beliefs, there are a number of studies which support aspects of Pollak's work. Campbell's work on female juvenile delinquency demonstrates that the official statistics, which put the ratio of male to female crime at approximately 6:1, are inaccurate. Her self-report study shows that the ratio of male to female juvenile crime was almost equal. Campbell claims that the disparity between the official crime statistics and the true rate of female juvenile crime arises because the police hold stereotypical images of women as law-abiding. Farrington and Kidd carried out an experiment in which they left letters (stamped but unposted) containing money in public places. Those who picked up the letters were observed and a note was made on whether they kept the letters or posted them. This experiment showed that women were just as likely to steal as men.

Although I criticise Pollak in this paragraph, you will notice that I quickly move on to evidence supporting the idea that agencies of social control are lenient towards women. It is easy to criticise the police and the courts for being biased towards women, but I think that many people are. For example, when I asked my students who was worse, Fred or Rosemary West, the majority said Rosemary, because she is a woman and didn't act in the way we expect women to act.

In support of the chivalry thesis, Farrington, this time working with Morris, found that women who were summoned to the magistrate's court were more likely than men to be let off with a fine or a caution. However, the work of Dobash and Dobash can be applied to offer a critique of the chivalry thesis. They found that when the woman is the victim of crime, such as rape or domestic violence, the courts are often harsh on her. Lees argues that in many instances the female rape victim is intimidated by the defence and made to feel as though she is on trial. Recently, the case of Julia Mason has been highlighted by women-fighting-for-justice groups after she experienced a six-day cross-examination in court by her attacker, who was defending himself. The notion that law-enforcement agencies are not chivalrous when the woman is the victim is further supported by Miller, who found that when instances of domestic violence were reported to the police, they were often reluctant to deal with the situation, viewing it as a domestic disturbance. Furthermore, Miller found that when the police did make an arrest, they were more likely to charge the violent male with disturbing the peace than with offences against the person.

Note how in this paragraph the essay takes a change in direction. The chivalry thesis comes under attack. I use examples of the rape trial to show that the courts are not always lenient towards women. Make sure you look out for other instances where women have been treated badly in court, and you can then substitute your own evidence in place of my suggestions.

Adler also challenges the chivalry thesis as an explanation of women's under-representation in the crime statistics. She believes that women are becoming more criminal owing to women's liberation. Adler looked at the changes in female crime in a number of different countries and found that it is on the increase. She claims that the reason for this change is that women are increasingly taking on men's roles, for example, becoming more involved in the labour market. Parallel to this development, women are increasingly involved in illegal activities. For Adler, this explains the recent rise in the official crime statistics for women.

You may like to apply a criticism which is based on the methodological approach of a writer. This is an easy way to pick up an evaluation mark or two and just goes to show you how important theory and method is as a part of your course. Once you know it, you can apply criticisms about validity, reliability and representativeness to almost every essay you do.

However, Adler has been criticised on methodological grounds. Her comparative cross-cultural study takes no account of cultural differences or the differences in legislation which govern each society. Above all, Adler has used the official statistics of some societies, which are not valid or reliable.

Another explanation for the reason women are under-represented in the crime statistics is that quite simply women do not commit as much crime as men. Carlen applies social control theory to explain why women are less criminal than males. She argues that working-class women make a 'class deal' and a 'gender deal'. Under the class deal women receive material rewards, which stem from gainful employment. Under the gender deal women receive both emotional and material rewards, which come from their partner's income and love. Both these types of reward result in the behaviour of women being controlled. Carlen argues that if these rewards are not on offer, for whatever reason, women are more likely to commit crime.

This paragraph introduces control theory as an explanation of why women commit less crime than men. Look back over the essay. Which theory do you think offers the best explanation of female criminality?

Heidensohn also believes that control theory explains why women commit fewer crimes than men. The housewife/mother role means that women have less opportunity for particular sorts of crime. This may be the reason that, although shoplifting is more common among young males than any other social group, it is the top crime for women. In their domestic role, this is one of the few crimes which women have the chance to commit. In addition, Heidensohn argues that females are controlled by the patriarchal society in which they live. For example, daughters tend to be given less freedom at night than sons, although it is more likely to be young men who are assaulted on the street. This factor also limits females' opportunity to commit crime. Heidensohn also claims that the self-image of women restricts their deviant behaviour because of the risk of being perceived as less than feminine. An aggressive woman, for example, is often referred to as a 'butch lesbian' if she challenges dominant male behaviour.

In conclusion, it is difficult to measure the true extent of female crime because the official statistics for all crimes, regardless of the perpetrator, are notoriously unreliable and can also be challenged on grounds of validity. Furthermore, as Smart argues, sociology and criminology are subjects which are dominated by men, and male sociologists tend to study male behaviour. Until this balance is redressed the extent of female criminality will continue to be something of a mystery.

> The essay concludes with an attack on the official crime statistics. This can be used in most essays on crime and deviance.

General Comments

The gender and crime debate is quite flexible in that, like many other essays, the information can be adapted and applied to a number of essay topics. For example, a lot of the information in this particular answer could be used to answer a question on crime statistics. Similarly, some of the information could be used to criticise the suggestion that crime is a working-class and male phenomenon.

Recently female crime has been under the spotlight, with the Rosemary West case and the Louise Woodward case. There have also been a number of television documentaries about the prevalence of female crime, for example Panorama's *Violent Women*. Keep your eye on current affairs so you can illustrate your work with up-to-date examples. The examiners credit this type of application as it shows that the student can make the link between theory and events in the real world.

Related questions

1   'The notion that women do not commit crime is a myth.' Discuss.

2   Assess the claim that crime is a working-class and a male phenomenon.

3   Examine the view that women commit less crime than men.

How have sociologists explained the persistence of
inequalities in health between the social classes?

Tackling the question

Note that the question presents the idea that there are persistent inequalities between the social classes as a fact. All the essay requires is an explanation of why these inequalities persist. So don't waste time discussing the inequalities themselves. Simple answers to this question will just focus on the cultural deprivation argument. In order to achieve a high grade you must also present a structuralist explanation of health inequalities. It is tempting to give common-sense arguments, but you must go beyond this. You should also look out for media reports which comment on the health of the nation, as you will be able to weave contemporary examples into your essay.

Answer

This paragraph just gives simple examples of class differences in health by referring to particular diseases.

Evidence concerning morbidity (that is, ill health due to disease) clearly shows that individuals in social class 5 (occupations such as labourer or cleaner) are far more likely to experience diseases of the heart and respiratory system than individuals in social class 1 (occupations such as accountant or solicitor). In addition, evidence on mortality shows that individuals from social class 1 are likely to live longer than those from social class 5.

In this paragraph I have set out the cultural deprivation argument. Weak students tend to drag this argument out into the realms of common sense. Do not do this if you want a higher grade.

According to the cultural deprivation argument, inequalities in health between social classes are due to individuals with ill health not leading healthy life styles, which in turn is a product of culture. This argument claims that the working class have different values from the middle class, and that these values lead to more illnesses and earlier death. There are four areas where these values can be demonstrated. Firstly, members of the working class tend to smoke more than the middle class, which means that they are prone to more bronchial and lung disorders, with the increased likelihood of premature death. On top of this, some of the working class are likely to live in poor accommodation which is often damp. This can further aggravate these complaints. Secondly, as Wilkinson shows, the poor tend to eat less fruit, vegetables, and fibre-rich food than other social groups. Diet is a major factor in health inequalities. Thirdly, Roberts argues that members of the working class are more likely to have sedentary leisure, whereas members of the middle class are more likely to adopt active leisure pursuits. Finally, the evidence suggests that members of the working class are less likely to take advantage of preventative health measures, such as ante-natal and post-natal clinics.

Proponents of the cultural deprivation approach would claim that the way to abolish inequalities in health between social classes is for working-class individuals to change their lifestyles. According to Edwina Currie (at one time Under-Secretary of State for Health), who had pointed to diet as a major factor in ill health, the answer was 'impressing upon people the need to look after themselves better'. Thus, for Currie, the sick can be blamed for their own ill health.

However, the major problem with the cultural deprivation argument is that it assumes that these cultural values are passed down from one generation to the next, when they could just as easily be caused by the economic circumstances of the poor. In other words, many of the poor cannot afford the healthy diet necessary for a healthy life style. A high-fibre loaf of bread in a major supermarket can cost more than twice as much as an economy white loaf. In addition, some members of the poorer sections of the community cannot afford to run a car. For example, only 14% of the residents of Everton, a poor area in Liverpool, run cars. It has been a major policy of large supermarket chains to locate outside urban areas, so many poor people cannot easily access these big supermarkets which are likely to have 'special offers' on food. Rather, many low-income groups are forced to shop at their local store where the products typically cost more, and are frequently sub-standard in terms of quality.

Another explanation for the persistence of inequalities in health between the social classes comes from Tudor-Hart, who claimed that working-class areas were frequently served by low-status GPs, whereas more successful GPs preferred to work in more prosperous areas which attracted better funding and better services. In addition, Tudor-Hart also argued that the distribution of resources within the National Health Service conforms to an 'inverse care law', where those whose need is less get more, while those whose need is greatest get less. However, this argument is flawed, as the unhealthiest part of Britain, which is Scotland, has traditionally received more funds than other areas.

The paragraph focuses on criticisms of the cultural deprivation argument. I have included an example of poverty from my local area to explain a point. I got this information from a local newspaper. You could scan your own local papers to see if you can find any information to apply to your sociology essays. Remember examiners award marks for links between theory and the real world.

In this paragraph I use a structuralist approach to evaluate the cultural deprivation theory. This moves the essay away from an almost commonsensical explanation to one which is academically more respectable.

Both of the explanations offered for the persistence of inequalities in health between the social classes would be dismissed by Marxists such as Doyal and Pennell, who would argue that health inequalities can only be understood by an analysis of capitalism. For Doyal and Pennell, the driving force behind capitalism is the pursuit of profit. This has a number of consequences on the health of the nation, and in particular the health of the working class. Firstly, work practices under capitalism lead to premature death among the working class through industrial accidents and industrial diseases. The death rate for those who worked in the construction industry 30 years ago is forecast to rise in the twenty-first century owing to the long-term effects of working with asbestos. In addition, the organisation of work under capitalism leads to stress for many workers. It is estimated that 56% of teachers retire early, many because of stress-related illnesses. Many more teachers want to retire early but are unable to do so because of financial considerations. The increase in bureaucracy and control which teachers face may have led to an increase in demand for early retirement since the late 1970s. Secondly, recent wage freezes and higher unemployment have resulted in increased material deprivation. It has been estimated that there are over 14 million individuals in Britain today who live in poverty. Old diseases, long considered eradicated, such as tuberculosis, are making a comeback in poor areas of cities such as Liverpool. Marxists point to two government-sponsored reports, *The Black Report* and *The Health Divide*, to substantiate this part of their argument. Both these reports indicate that poverty is the chief cause of poor health. Townsend and Phillimore conclude that the health gap is a consequence of the wealth gap. It is important to note that both of these reports, although commissioned by the government, were never published. Thirdly, Marxists point to the economic power of the large medical corporations which ensures that their interests are served first and foremost. Due to changes in National Health Service provision there is increasing emphasis on private medicine through health insurance and the construction of private hospitals. Marxists would argue that equality of health is unlikely to happen under the capitalist system.

Some would argue that to blame capitalism for ill health is too simple, as even more severe health and welfare problems existed in the former 'communist' Eastern bloc countries (though contemporary Western Marxists would not see any of these countries as socialist).

Nevertheless, the pursuit of profit under capitalism has been responsible for great advances in medical technology. However, if medical companies which are in direct competition with one another, co-operated and shared their knowledge, then the world

Do not be fooled into thinking that the health of the population is the major concern of drug companies. They are in it for profit.

might be a step closer to curing cancer and AIDS. It can be argued that the shareholders in the company which makes the breakthrough in the cure for cancer or AIDS, will become incredibly wealthy.

Illich dismisses the notion that advances in medical technology are the major cause of better health for the nation in general. He claims that health started to improve for all social classes with better living conditions, sanitation and diet. It can be argued that fresh running water in the home and sewage systems have done more for the health of the nation than any piece of medical technology. McKeown, in his historical study of Western societies, also claims that diet is a key factor in improving health. He shows that even rationing in the Second World War improved the health of the British working class, as families were encouraged to grow and eat their own vegetables. In addition, as a result of rationing, people tended to eat less fat. However, Save the Children reports that 40% of the residents of Everton, in Liverpool, suffer long-term illnesses. The inhabitants have to walk about two miles in order to buy fresh food. Sixty-seven per cent of the households in the area have no working adult. This might lead some to claim that improvements in living conditions are being eroded for certain sections of the population. Merseyside is seen as so poor that it ranks alongside third world countries and thus attracts grants from the European Union.

This paragraph starts by looking at diet as a key factor in the health of the nation. Note that the example of Everton has been applied again in this section of the essay. However, previously I used information about car ownership, whereas this time I have picked out and applied the information which relates to the number of residents who suffer from disease and unemployment. Do not be afraid to use the same piece of research twice in one essay, just be careful to avoid repetition.

This essay concludes that the persistence in health inequalities between the social classes is due to structured inequalities within society as a whole. Those groups with low incomes are unable to buy themselves healthy lifestyles. Dorling, of Bristol University, claims that each £100 rise in annual income could give a low-paid worker nine extra days of life.

General comments

Knowledge concerning the health of the nation can be applied in poverty essays. In addition, the same information can be adapted for essays on race and health, and gender and health. As stated, for this essay I used examples from my local environment. This information was reported in my local paper. Keep your eyes and ears open for reports which you can use for examples in your work. Essays become much stronger if you can link social theory to an event or present-day statistic.

Related questions

1 Evaluate sociological explanations for differential levels of health between social classes.

2 'The introduction of the National Health Service has done little to eradicate inequalites in health.' What explanations have sociologists given for this?

3 Evaluate the statement that poor health is caused by poverty.

Assess the view that third world countries are
underdeveloped simply because first world
countries are developed.

Tackling the question

The question here takes its theme from dependency theory which is based on Marxism.
Therefore, in order to achieve the higher mark bands you will have to address the main
issues within dependency theory. You may come across arguments which frown upon the
use of the term 'third world'. Some sociologists believe that you should use the term
'developing countries'. I disagree with this because, as this essay will show you, the notion
that these countries are developing is often a misconception.

A**nswer**

Guidance notes

Third world countries such as Costa Rica, Bolivia, Chad and
Vietnam are generally found in South and Central America, Africa
and Asia. They tend to be characterised by widespread poverty,
illiteracy, lack of health-care facilities and low economic growth.
In comparison, first world countries such as the United States of
America and the United Kingdom are found in North America and
Western Europe. First world countries tend to use most of the
world's resources, and are characterised by what Veblen called
'conspicuous consumption'.

In this introductory paragraph I
distinguish between first world
countries and third world
countries. Note that I have also
provided suitable examples.

Modernisation theorists, such as Rostow, see the underdevelopment of third world countries as a result of lack of economic and
social progression. Rostow argues that, in order to develop,
societies must pass through five evolutionary stages. He argues
that third world countries need to have science, technology and
capital investment before industrialisation can occur. Parsons and
Hoselitz agree with Rostow, but they also stress the importance
of cultural change. They argue that for underdeveloped third world
countries to become developed, they must undergo a change in

One of the major problems
students have with modernisation
theory is that they write far too
much, which results in an
unbalanced essay as they can run
out of time. One reason for

writing too much is trying to remember Rostow's five stages of development. There is no need for this as long as you give the gist of Rostow's argument.

This is the start of dependency theory as specified in the title. Note how it links back to the question in the very first sentence.

Here is an example of coffee which is grown in poor countries but which is processed and marketed by first world companies for vast profits.

values. The traditional values of tribal systems, such as collectivism and ascribed status, which are often found in third world countries, are frequently obstacles to development. Modernisation theorists believe that third world countries are underdeveloped because they lack material investment and appropriate cultural values.

In contrast, dependency theorists such as Frank, who mainly use a Marxist analysis, claim that third world countries are underdeveloped simply because first world countries are developed. According to this theory, first world countries such as the United Kingdom have developed at the expense of third world countries. In other words, wealthy countries have caused poor countries to be poor. There are five main reasons for this. One put forward by advocates of dependency theory is that a number of developed societies, like Britain, became successful partly because of the slave trade. Without the slave trade, Britain's cotton industry would not have been successful. Britain was able to base its cotton industry on the products of the plantations of the southern states of America, which had little in the way of labour costs. However, some developed countries, such as Sweden, became successful without the slave trade.

Another reason dependency theorists put forward to explain the weak position of third world countries is that many Western European countries had colonies which they were able to exploit. Britain exploited India, amongst other countries, just as France exploited Indo-China (Vietnam). Colonialism created a pattern of dependency which still exists today. Third world countries owe massive debts to the World Bank and the International Monetary Fund. Frank calls this 'bondage'. He argues that modernisation theorists ignore these two important influences which help to explain why third world countries are underdeveloped. Caulfield claims that the World Bank is incompetent because it frequently funds projects which are not financially sound. As a result of the World Bank's bad decisions, the borrowing country is often forced to take out yet another loan, thus increasing its debts. According to Caulfield, the World Bank profits more from its failed projects than its successes.

The third reason put forward by dependency theorists is that the international trading system puts third world countries at a disadvantage within the world market. Third world countries tend to rely on primary products such as coffee, from which there is little money to be made in their raw state. Most of the money made from coffee goes to large corporations such as Nestlé and General Foods. The countries which produce the coffee beans make relatively little from the product.

Fourthly, dependency theorists argue that transnational corporations help to keep third world countries underdeveloped. Gortz shows that more than one quarter of the most fertile of third world land is monopolised by Western transnational corporations, to meet the West's fashion and food 'needs'. For example, 50% of Ghana's land is given over to cocoa production. On the other hand, modernisation theorists point to the importance of transnational corporations in creating employment in underdeveloped societies. However, as Hayter argues, most jobs created by transnational corporations in third world countries are for semi-skilled and unskilled workers. The highly paid jobs tend to go to first world expatriates, as is the case with Honda in Brazil, and Volkswagen in Mexico. In support of this point, Myrdal shows that there is a net flow of money from third world countries to first world countries.

Finally, dependency theorists such as Hayter consider the role of aid in keeping third world countries tied to developed countries. Most loans from first world countries are tied, often to the purchase of military hardware – for example, the sale by the United Kingdom of Hawk aircraft to Indonesia. At the present time, Indonesia is seeking another loan from the International Monetary Fund. In addition, many aid projects are completely irrelevant to the majority of the local people, and the money for these aid projects goes back to companies in the donor country, as is the case with the Pergau Dam in Malaysia which, although paid for with British aid, was also built by British companies. Aid is frequently used as a political weapon to support friendly third world governments.

Some critics of dependency theory, such as Robinson, argue that for third world countries some development, or dependent development, is better than no development at all. In addition, the critics claim that dependency theory does not explain the success of Pacific rim countries such as South Korea and Malaysia – though it should be pointed out that in 1997 a number of these Pacific rim countries began to experience severe economic and financial problems. Despite these criticisms of dependency theory, it offers a good understanding of why third world countries continue to be underdeveloped through their continuing relationship with first world countries.

Next time you are in your local supermarket see if you can find another product from a poorer country which you can use as your own example. Remember: to write a good sociology essay, you've got to think sociologically.

This paragraph discusses aid and uses the example of the supply of British Aerospace Hawk aircraft to Indonesia. Britain has been known to supply tanks, missiles and guns to other countries. The Labour government claims that it will change this aid policy. You should monitor developments on this front.

General comments

On occasion you will find that this question uses the terms 'the north' to refer to developed countries and 'the south' to refer to underdeveloped countries. Recent textbooks also use these terms. The material you use to answer the question is just the same no matter what terms are used.

Related questions

1 Aid is often cited as a factor leading to continuing dependency. How far can this explain the underdevelopment of third world countries?

2 'Modernisation theory has failed to produce an adequate explanation of underdevelopment.' Discuss.

3 To what extent is it true to say that transnational corporations contribute little to the development of poor countries?

Question 27

'Those in poverty have only themselves
to blame.' Discuss.

Tackling the question

Essays on poverty tend to focus on one of three issues – the persistence of poverty, the definition of poverty and explanations for poverty. There are many theories which can be applied to this particular essay question. The major concern is that there is too much material to choose from, so it may be a good idea to draw up an essay plan which you can use to guide you through the essay-writing process. For this essay, you must be aware that the statement which makes up this essay is typical of New Right sociology. It would be difficult to score highly on this essay without this knowledge.

Answer

Guidance notes

According to Townsend's statistics on poverty, over 14 million individuals live in relative poverty in Britain today. For some commentators, notably the New Right, those who live in poverty only have themselves to blame. This essay will assess this assertion.

I have opened the essay by mentioning Townsend's estimate of the numbers in poverty. It is important to remember that this estimate is for those living in relative poverty, not absolute poverty. If you can remember a specific statistic like this it can provide a good starting point for an essay.

Throughout the ages, those living in poverty have often been blamed for their own situation. In other words, if individuals live in poverty, it is their own fault. This is known as the 'individualistic' theory of poverty and was popular as early as the nineteenth century. Spencer, an early sociologist who wrote from this perspective, suggested that poverty was self-inflicted. He argued against supplying financial help for the poor because he believed that it would result in the poor becoming dependent on this money. He claimed that financial help would discourage the poor from helping themselves and encourage them to lead easy, lazy lives. Spencer did not advocate eradicating poverty, but argued that poverty was needed in society because it gave individuals the incentive to work. Spencer used the term 'survival of the fittest' to justify his position. He believed that the successful and hard-working should keep their rewards while the weak should be left alone to fight their way out of a life of poverty.

This paragraph uses the work of Spencer to show that there is a long-standing tradition of blaming the poor for their own poverty.

The notion that the poor are to blame for their own situation has been resurrected in recent years by the New Right. The New Right position supports Spencer because, like Spencer, the New Right apportion some of the blame for poverty to those who actually live in it, but they put most of the blame on the welfare state. The New Right believe that Spencer's warning about what would happen if the state intervened in the lives of the poor has come to pass. They argue that the welfare state is responsible for creating a culture of dependency and as a result the welfare state should be dismantled, so that individuals will be encouraged to stand on their own two feet. According to the New Right perspective, the welfare state is a drain on the economy. They argue that the money spent on welfare provision in Britain should be redirected into the economy via tax reductions, where it would create more jobs. They believe that boosting the economy would do more to alleviate poverty than the welfare state has ever done, and argue that individuals should take out individual insurance policies to cover themselves against medical costs and other services provided by the welfare state. This view is open to criticism. One country which does not have a comprehesive welfare state is the United States. However, the United States does have high levels of poverty, and, as a consequence some suggest, high levels of crime.

Nevertheless, according to Marsland, the welfare state facilitates a culture of dependency which effectively encourages the poor to stay poor. He argues that Britain is in a situation where the poor do not want to work because the welfare state is providing for their physical needs. He does not advocate that the welfare state should be completely scrapped, but believes that all benefits should be means-tested and only those not capable of work, such as the sick and the disabled, should be entitled to welfare benefits.

Note that within this paragraph I have used Jordan to criticise the New Right. I have also included information on the Labour government's problematic 'back to work' policy. Obviously, policies do change, especially when they are controversial. Make sure you keep up to date with policy changes in this area.

Jordan criticises the views of the New Right and Marsland, arguing that many individuals who live in poverty and claim state benefits want to find work. Jordan says that too often they are held back from taking jobs because the wages which are on offer are so low that they would not allow an adequate standard of living. Recent evidence published by the Labour government about the controversial issue of putting single mothers on back-to-work programmes also suggests that individuals on state benefits would ideally like to work. Dean and Taylor-Gooby support Jordan. They conducted research which involved 85 in-depth interviews with individuals claiming welfare benefits. They found that only four of their sample did not want to work. It appears that there is little evidence to suggest that those living in poverty only have themselves to blame. It is more likely that low wages do not provide an incentive for individuals to return to work.

As stated in the introduction, Townsend says that over 14 million individuals live in relative poverty in Britain today. This represents over a fifth of the population. Evidence suggests that certain groups in society are more likely to be found in this group than others. Ethnic minorities, the sick and disabled, people claiming benefits and the elderly are disproportionately represented in this figure. The elderly cannot help being old, just as the sick and disabled cannot help their physical condition, so it is difficult to imagine how these groups are to blame for their own poverty. Furthermore, evidence from the report, *Low Income Statistics: Low Income Families*, shows an emergence of a new category of individuals who live below the poverty line, that is low-paid full-time workers. The report claims that there is an increasing number of full-time workers who take home less than the basic unemployment rate. Therefore, the notion that people who live in poverty have only themselves to blame can be refuted.

> This paragraph provides some excellent evidence about the poor in Britain.

Some sociologists blame poverty on government and policy makers. It can be argued that successive governments have systematically introduced policies which have weakened the position of the poor while strengthening the position of the rich. An example of this is the introduction of the poll tax/council tax. Before the days of the poll tax, individuals living in council houses only made a small contribution to housing rates which was included in the cost of the weekly rent. However, when the poll tax was introduced, many individuals found themselves paying hefty bills. The low paid were particularly affected because they did not receive a discount on their payment. It is possible that this one social policy pushed many individuals below the poverty line. Many people had to cut back on essentials in order to meet this new household bill. On the other hand, those who lived in large houses in expensive areas, who had paid up to £2000 a year in rates, paid much less under the poll tax, as the rate for the highest band was around £1000 a year. This government policy made the poor poorer and the rich richer, and can be used as evidence against the suggestion that the poor are to blame for their own condition.

> In this paragraph I have taken the essay in a different direction. This time attention focuses on government policy as a cause of poverty. I have used the example of the poll tax/council tax to make my point. Obviously there are many other examples that could have been used, but one is enough to illustrate the point. The inherent danger in taking up this line of argument is that the essay can turn into a political soap box.

The last Conservative government was particularly criticised for its social policy which in effect made the poor poorer. In March 1997, Peter Lilley introduced regulations cutting housing benefit to young people, which resulted in individuals under the age of 25 only receiving enough benefit to afford a single room in a shared house. This is in an era when homelessness among the young is an ever-increasing problem. In addition, Lilley introduced changes to the funeral grant. The changes deny poor families assistance with funeral costs unless they can prove that every member of their direct family is claiming benefits. This means that at a time of great upset, these impoverished families will be subjected to intrusive questioning. Furthermore, single mothers are now denied assistance with the cost of their child's funeral if the father of the child is traceable and is not claiming benefits. It has been estimated that this change alone will save an estimated 4 million pounds a year. It could be argued that government policy does not just exacerbate poverty but actually creates it.

I have introduced Marxism to explain why poverty has an important place in capitalism. I have also applied the work of Golding and Middleton to explain this complex point. Although I have used a quote in this paragraph, you will not be expected to remember quotes under examination conditions. As long as you get down the gist of what the sociologist is saying you'll be fine.

Marxists would argue that poverty is functional to capitalism as it not only provides an incentive to work, but can also be used to divide the working class. For example, those in poverty are often seen as scroungers who are costing the nation a fortune. Golding and Middleton conducted a content analysis study of press output with regard to the poor. They found that a disproportionate amount of space was given over to stories concerning social security fraud, alleged over-generosity and illegitimate welfare claims. No comment was made about the fact that millions of pounds worth of benefit go unclaimed every year. Golding and Middleton quote a famous article which appeared in the *Daily Mail* in 1976. The article entitled 'Scroungers by the Sea' claimed that 'seaside social security offices were thick with subsidised cigarette smoke, the smell of alcohol paid for by the state and the smugly tanned faces of the leeches feeding off the hard-working ordinary silent majority'. Golding and Middleton also found that stories involving social security fraud were nearly always given front page headlines whereas tax evasion, which costs the state about 100 times more than social security fraud, was hardly ever commented on.

The conclusion summarises the main theories which have been examined in the essay.

In conclusion, the evidence which has been presented demonstrates that the poor are not to blame for their own situation. The elderly cannot help being old, just as the sick and disabled cannot help being sick and disabled. Furthermore, evidence suggests that unemployed individuals living in poverty do want to work. It appears that most individuals living on benefits would trade their impoverished position for a decent job with decent pay. Unfortunately, the chances of achieving a good job seem highly unlikely for most, as poverty among the young unemployed can usually be correlated with poor educational qualifications and poor skills.

General Comments

Poverty is a very emotive subject. Be careful that your essay doesn't read like a crusade. It is interesting to note that some of the theories of poverty which are typically used in essays looking at the persistence of poverty can also be also used in this type of essay.

Related questions

1 'The welfare state has created a culture of dependency.' Discuss.

2 How far is it true to say that government policy of recent years has exacerbated poverty rather than helped to eradicate it?

3 In what ways does a concept of underclass add to our understanding of poverty?

Question 28

How far is it true to say that the poor will always be with us?

Tackling the question

This essay demands that you know quite a lot about the introduction of the welfare state. Within the essay, you will be expected to judge whether the welfare state has achieved its aims or whether the poor will always have a place in British society. It is fairly easy to find contemporary evidence on poverty which you can apply to support your points. Remember, if the essay title takes the form of a question you must make sure you provide an answer.

Answer

In the opening paragraph I have given a brief introduction to the welfare state and its aims. Note that I tie the information back to the essay title at the end of the paragraph and hence, answer the question.

In 1945, as a result of the Beveridge Report, the welfare state was introduced to Britain. The welfare state was introduced to remedy five problems or evils which Beveridge identified as afflicting British society. These were: 'squalor', by which he meant poor housing; 'idleness', or unemployment; 'disease', or poor health; 'ignorance', which Beveridge used to refer to poor educational standards; and 'want', or poverty. The objective adopted by the then government was that individuals should be protected from these five evils from the 'cradle to the grave'. The funding for the welfare state came from a system of national insurance, which was an attempt at redistributing income from the most well-off to the least well-off. However, it is over 50 years since the welfare state was introduced to Britain, yet the five evils, and in particular poverty, still exist to some extent in British society. It could be argued that if the welfare state cannot eradicate poverty, then it is probable that the poor will always be with us.

According to Townsend, in Britain today there are over 14 million individuals living in relative poverty. This is over a fifth of the population. It would appear then that the welfare state has not been successful in its quest to eradicate poverty in Britain, and this had led some commentators to argue that the poor will always be with us.

Several reasons have been put forward to explain the persistence of poverty in British society. The New Right have blamed the welfare state itself. According to Marsland, the welfare state discourages individuals from standing on their own two feet. Marsland has advocated that state benefits only be payable to individuals who are physically unable work. Marsland and other New Right commentators suggest that the welfare state has created a culture of dependency and it is the existence of the welfare state itself which accounts for the persistence of poverty. They believe that poverty will only start to disappear once the welfare state has been dismantled.

Another explanation of why poverty is still a problem in British society has been put forward by Oscar Lewis. Lewis claims that there is a culture of poverty which is passed down from generation to generation. The culture of poverty includes fatalistic attitudes – many individuals accept poverty as a way of life and do not try to escape from it. According to Lewis, the poor are alienated from wider society and must therefore find methods of coping. These methods of coping become so intrinsic, and are so well practised, that they become a way of life. As a result, a culture of poverty is created. Lewis is supported by Halsey, who sees poverty as a subculture. Halsey states that the poor are different from other social groups because they have had to adapt to the conditions of poverty in which they live, and that this subculture of poverty is passed from one generation to another.

A concept similar to the culture of poverty is that of the cycle of deprivation. Commentators such as Keith Joseph (former Conservative minister) have used the cycle of deprivation to explain the persistence of poverty in British society. Joseph criticised the child-rearing techniques of the poor, claiming that these led their offspring to be emotionally, socially and intellectually deprived. This led to failure in the education system, and subsequently to unskilled jobs or unemployment. Joseph argued that this in turn would lead the offspring of the poor to have unstable family lives as adults, which would then lead them to be inadequate parents. Joseph argued that this vicious circle is a product of values and attitudes passed down from one generation to the next. In his own words, Joseph claims that this creates 'a culture of dependency'.

The culture of poverty and the cycle of deprivation are similar in that they both take the view that families transmit the values associated with poverty from one generation to the next. However, both of these theories can be criticised. Both Lewis and Joseph use stereotyped notions of the poor and consequently make generalisations about their behaviour and attitudes. Neither of the theories put forward attempts to explain how the behaviour and

In this paragraph I offer a New Right explanation for the persistence of poverty. You will notice that the next paragraph is given over to the 'culture of poverty' perspective and the following paragraph is spent explaining the cycle of deprivation. This means that the essay is highly structured. This makes it easier for the reader and easier for you, the student, to revise.

This paragraph is used to criticise two approaches. Note how it points to the similarities in the two theories.

attitudes associated with poverty started in the first place. Furthermore, neither of the approaches takes into account that some children born into poverty will escape from poverty as adults, while some not born into poverty will fall into poverty as adults, despite having had economically stable childhoods.

Notice how the language used at the beginning of this paragraph changes the direction of the poverty debate. It is important to use good link words, phrases and sentences. This allows the essay to flow rather than reading like a load of notes strung together.

The theories which have been explored so far have put forward the view that the poor can be identified by personality traits – they are lazy, unwilling to work and bad parents. Treating poverty as a subculture in this way creates *laissez-faire* attitudes towards the poor. As a result there is less pressure on officials to do anything to alleviate poverty. Even if the persistence of poverty was caused by a culture or a cycle of poverty, there is hardly ever any mention of finding ways to break the cycle. Miliband criticises the notion of a culture of poverty. He argues that if such a thing exists then it is an induced culture which has been deliberately manipulated to give rise to feelings of guilt and passivity.

In addition, it can be argued that the cycle of deprivation and the culture of poverty explanations do not look at adverse external forces which act against the poor. The structuralist approach takes this into account and arguably offers a more plausible explanation of why the poor are still with us after 50 years of the welfare state.

So far the theories put forward have been fairly easy to understand. At this point in the essay a Marxist analysis of poverty is used. Stronger candidates should be able to do this. Try to remember that the key issue here is that poverty serves to divide the working class. Think of it like football. Sometimes people fall out because they support two different football teams, e.g. relationships between Liverpool and Manchester United supporters tend not to be the closest in the world. In this case one group of people look down their noses at another group of people. The same is true of poverty, some people don't like others just because they 'sign on'. This is really serious for

In a class-divided society such as Britain, there are vast disparities between the rich and poor in terms of income, wealth and power. It can be argued that poverty is functional to this system of inequalities, as it is the bedrock on which inequalities rest. In Britain today, there is sufficient income and wealth to eradicate poverty, but poverty actually maintains wealth, and in particular, extreme wealth. Holman argues that the function of poverty is to maintain the status quo. According to Jordan, and Westergaard and Resler, poverty is a device which is used to create divisions between the proletariat. The working class is divided into two groups, the respectable working class and the claiming class. The latter are often regarded as scroungers and layabouts. The proletariat is then fragmented, often with the 'respectable' working class feeling bitter towards the 'claiming' sector of the working class. The dominant ideology in British society is that income and wealth come from hard work and ability, and the 'claiming' section of the working class is often portrayed as having the opposite characteristics. Marxists see poverty as serving the function of dividing the working class so that it will never be united. The overthrow of capitalism as predicted by Marx is dependent on the working class coming together and achieving class-consciousness. While the working class is divided, the position of élites is legitimised. It may be that if the position of the poor was considered unjust, then other positions on the social scale might be looked into and their legitimacy questioned.

According to Miliband, the poor will always be with us because they face not only economic deprivation caused by the unequal structure of society, but also political deprivation. Miliband claims that there are conflicting forces operating within society. Some forces make for the persistence of poverty, while others work against it. According to Miliband, improvements in the circumstances of the poor require public expenditure. However, the public purse has limited amounts of money and there are a lot of powerful people and groups making claims on this money. Money from the National Lottery, for example, has been used for restoring the Royal Opera House. Miliband argues that projects which benefit the wealthy are given priority and are legitimised by governments, because, as Marx suggested, any government is the management committee for the affairs of the whole bourgeoisie. The groups supporting the poor – such a Shelter and the Child Poverty Action Group – enter this market from a weak position. They face an uphill struggle in trying to create greater social awareness about poverty and are systematically opposed by parts of the mass media and right-wing politicians like Peter Lilley, who do their best to portray people who claim welfare benefits as scroungers. Poverty tends to be treated with suspicion.

In conclusion, this essay has demonstrated that the poor are still with us despite over 50 years of the welfare state. For New Right commentators such as Marsland, poverty will not even start to be eroded until welfare provision is withdrawn from individuals physically fit enough to work. However, for commentators such as Lewis and Joseph, poverty will always be with us because it has developed its own subculture which is passed down from generation to generation. Meanwhile, for Marxists such as Miliband, poverty will always be with us while we have a capitalist society. Marxists believe that poverty serves to maintain the status quo and legitimise the position of the wealthy. The division of the working class makes it extremely unlikely that the proletariat will ever develop the class-consciousness or indeed the desire to overthrow capitalism in favour of a new epoch of socialism. Careful analysis of the theories and of contemporary society suggests that the poor will always be with us.

Marxists because you can't have a revolution if the people are not on the same side.

In this paragraph I have brought in the power differences between groups who support the poor and other pressure groups. The National Lottery is useful for explaining the point because it is contemporary and controversial. Remember that just around the corner from the Royal Opera House, some people are living in cardboard boxes. Do be careful not to go on a political crusade in your answer, no matter how much you are tempted.

The concluding paragraph sums up the evidence and comments that it is unlikely that poverty will ever disappear. Remember to answer the question.

General comments

This essay question is really important in sociology because it confronts the issue of poverty rather than trying to disguise it through the use of terms such as 'underclass'. However, you must not take this to mean that you have licence to launch into an essay full of political diatribe. I know that poverty is an emotive subject but you must keep your feelings out of your essays.

You will find that there is a great deal of overlap on questions about poverty and questions on the underclass. Those groups said to be in the underclass are the same groups that live in poverty, so a lot of the information is interchangeable. You will also note that theories used in the previous poverty essay can be used to explain the persistence of poverty. However, because there is so much information make sure you plan your work carefully or you may find that you have too much to fit into a 45 minute essay.

Related questions

1   Despite 50 years of the welfare state, poverty is still a prominent feature of British society. What explanations have sociologists offered for this phenomenon?

2   Discuss the notion that Britain has an ethnically-differentiated underclass.

3   Evaluate the suggestion that there has been a feminisation of poverty in modern British society.

Question 29

'The major factor influencing gender roles is the mass media.' Discuss this statement.

Tackling the question

This is a question which requires reference to a range of research examining different types of mass media. My answer looks at children's books, comics, women's magazines and television advertising, but you could choose different aspects of the media for your answer. Poor answers to this question will agree with the statement. If you think about the proposition, it is obvious that socialisation is the major factor influencing gender roles, not the mass media. Your essay will need to reflect this, but also show that the mass media play a role in reinforcing gender roles. In sociology think hard before you agree with anything!

Answer

Guidance notes

According to Trowler, the mass media can be defined as 'the methods and organisations used by specialist social groups to convey messages to large, socially mixed and widely dispersed audiences'. The mass media can be said to include television, film, the national press, music, videos, magazines, and computer games.

> I have put in a definition of the mass media plus a number of examples, but under exam conditions you should skip this definition unless the question is phrased 'what do you understand by...'. You might like to include some ideas about gender roles in your opening paragraph.

A number of studies of the mass media have expressed concern about the media's portrayal of gender roles. According to McRobbie, the media can be particularly criticised for their portrayal of the gender roles of women. McRobbie claims that the way in which women are presented is both limited and limiting. In other words, the media present women in only a few roles, such as housewife, mother, appendages to men's arms or sexual playthings. According to McRobbie, the limited number of female gender roles which the media put across may lead many women to believe that only a limited number of roles are open to them. This may well have an effect on the self-image and aspirations of females. The same does not apply to male gender roles.

> In this paragraph I show how the mass media present female gender roles, and I refer to male gender roles.

In order to develop logic and coherence, I start with one of the earliest forms of media that many children are exposed to, young children's books. You might like to find a range of contemporary books for young children from something like the Oxford Reading Scheme to see if there has been any change in the content.

Individuals in society are exposed to a range of mass media throughout their lifetimes, and it is therefore inevitable that the mass media will have some influence over individuals' attitudes and beliefs. Exposure to the mass media starts at an early age, as does exposure to gender stereotypes. This is demonstrated in the work of a number of writers, including Sharpe, Lobban and Best, who have pointed to the representations of gender roles of males and females in the reading material of young children. These three separate studies found that young children's books contained gender stereotypes. Sharpe, Lobban and Best all found that females were portrayed by the books as passive and dependent, whereas males were more likely to be portrayed as active and independent. When occupational roles were shown these were also likely to be stereotyped with, for example, males being portrayed as doctors while females were portrayed as nurses.

This is an important opening sentence which links to the question and refutes the statement.

However, none of these studies claims that the mass media cause gender roles or gender stereotypes, rather that they reinforce existing attitudes to gender. Sharpe also examined children's comics and found that comics endorsed the traditional gender roles as well. This research is supported by Adams and Laurikietis, who argue that comics for boys are about 'bravery and adventure' and contain 'no girls, or if they do appear, their part in the story is insignificant'. The media aimed at children reinforce traditional gender roles.

The potential of the mass media for influencing gender roles can also be seen in Ferguson's analysis of the content of the women's magazines, *Woman*, *Woman's Own* and *Woman's Weekly* for the period 1949–74. She found that two dominant themes ran through all the magazines she analysed. Firstly, the importance of love and 'getting a man', and secondly, the value of self-improvement. In her follow-up study of magazines for 1979–80, Ferguson found that the theme of self-improvement had become dominant, but the importance of love and getting a man was still a significant part of the content. Within her analysis, Ferguson identified a 'cult of femininity' which promoted the ideals of the family, marriage, the domestic role, and appearance. As Sharpe argues, the effect of these magazines is to exclude any concept of happiness in the world outside the home. However, over recent years there has been a new trend in women's magazines, including *Marie-Claire*, *Cosmopolitan*, and *New Woman*, to name but a few. These magazines are supposed to represent a new genre, in that they focus on career women. However, they all place a strong emphasis on having a man, getting a man, and keeping a man. Gender roles are still being stereotyped by this form of mass media.

Since Ferguson carried out her research, there has also been a plethora of new publications aimed at men, for example, *GQ* and *FHM* which, it might be argued, celebrate and encourage a 'cult of masculinity'. Certainly, the mass media themselves have identified at least two masculine stereotypes, that is 'laddishness', as found in the sitcom, *Men Behaving Badly*, and the caring, sensitive 'new man', who, according to feminist research, is a mythical character.

An overlap with Ferguson's work can be found in the world of advertising, with its emphasis on 'feminine perfection'. (The ideal of feminine perfection does after all support a large fashion and beauty industry.) According to Dominick and Rauch, the subordinate position of women is reflected and reinforced through the advertising industry. In a study of television advertising, Dominick and Rauch found that more than half of the representations of women were in the housewife/mother role. In addition, they found that advertisers tend to use young attractive women to sell their products, especially to men. Dominick and Rauch found that 71% of women in advertising were aged between 20 and 35. In many cases women are portrayed as sexual objects, such as in the Peugeot 'nice car – want to show me what it can do' advert. A more recent advert which uses stereotypical images of gender is the Fiat advert, where the young male and young female go into the woman's father's study and look at the car on the computer. The young man takes over the operating of the computer and proceeds to talk about the technical aspects of the car. The woman's contribution to the advert is to mention the stereo. This is a perfect example of how the mass media play a role in reinforcing gender stereotypes.

More recent research by Bretl and Cantor based on American television advertisements has found some differences between British and American advertising. In the USA males and females are used more or less equally as the main characters in prime-time television adverts. Nevertheless, their research still showed support for Dominick and Rauch, in that they found that males were more likely to be found in higher-status and more dominant occupations than females. Research such as this has led Root to argue that the images of women which are portrayed by the media are symbolic. She claims that in some cases 'the potential buyer is being asked to bask in the agreeable sensation of power and control which images of near-naked women suggest to men in this society'. According to Root, the same messages, that women are for male enjoyment and that they are sexually available, are found in pornography.

This section looks at new publications directed mainly at males so that the essay does not look just at female stereotypes.

The conclusion brings in other factors which may affect gender roles to show that the mass media do not operate in isolation. It also makes a methodological point about carrying out research on this topic.

In conclusion, the research quoted shows that the mass media are a factor in influencing gender roles, in that they tend to reinforce stereotypical gender images. However, none of the research identifies the mass media as the major factor in creating gender roles. It would be difficult to construct an experiment or a research project to test the hypothesis that the mass media are a major influence on gender roles. It can be argued that the most important influence on gender roles is the socialisation process. In Western societies it is fairly typical for male babies to be dressed in blue, bought toys which can be seen as symbolic of aggression, and played with in a fairly rough manner. Meanwhile female children tend to be dressed in pink, bought pink things, encouraged to take care of their appearance, and so on. The difference in socialisation patterns between male and female children makes children susceptible to the gender stereotypes which the media reinforce. Nevertheless, despite these factors, there are a number of influences in contemporary Britain which attempt to counteract stereotypical gender roles. Modern Britain is seeing the emergence of the successful female in terms of educational achievement, and evidence suggests that more and more women are focusing on a career rather than marriage and babies. However, it is likely that these women have just put off marriage and motherhood until their thirties, so it could be argued that women still succumb to the stereotyped role eventually.

General comments

There are a number of essays on the media which involve discussions revolving around the notion that the media can cause behaviour, beliefs, attitudes or tastes. Before tackling any of these questions read Klapper's work on mass communication, which will help you to avoid accepting such assertions uncritically.

Related questions

1   'Media representations of women are distortions of reality.' Examine this view.

2   'The media must have some effect on gender roles, but this does not happen in isolation.' Discuss.

3   Assess the extent to which the media reflect the position of women in modern British society.

Question 30

How far is it true to say that managers in the
mass media are primarily responsible for the
output of the media?

Tackling the question

The debate concerning ownership and control in the mass media is an 'old chestnut'. It requires a good understanding of a well-known sociological debate between Marxists on the one hand and managerial revolution theorists and pluralists on the other hand. Some students are put off by the term 'managerial revolution thesis' which you will find in textbooks. In reality, it is simple – all it means is that in modern society managers run large companies because the owners do not have the technical skill to run them. Once you grasp this then it becomes fairly simple to cover this debate.

Answer

Guidance notes

According to Giddens, the mass media are 'forms of communication such as newspapers, magazines, radio and television, designed to reach mass audiences'. The tendency for the ownership of the mass media to be concentrated in the hands of a few owners has met with alarm in some sections of society. Particular concern has been expressed about Rupert Murdoch's massive global multimedia conglomerate. Murdoch owns or has holdings in Twentieth Century Fox (USA), Vox Satellite (Germany), the *Sun*, the *News of the World*, the *Times*, the *Sunday Times*, *BSkyB* and Harper Collins publishers (the UK). In Asia, he has holdings in Star Satellite which covers India, China, Japan and other countries. Finally, he has holdings in various newspapers in Australia. Marxists have claimed that such concentration of ownership limits media freedom and that ownership inevitably affects the content of mass media output. According to Marxists, those who own and control the means of production also control the flow of ideas in society. Marx claimed that the ruling ideas of any epoch are the ideas of the ruling class. However, Dahrendorf would argue that the ruling class that Marx was writing about has broken up, and shareholding is now more widespread than it was in the nineteenth century. This argument is supported by Saunders. Both Dahrendorf

In this opening paragraph, I illustrate the patterns of media ownership by referring to the Murdoch empire. You will need to keep an eye on this because ownership within the mass media is constantly changing. By the time this book is published, the material I have written on Murdoch's holdings may be out of date. Finally, in this paragraph I map out the answer by stating the main positions in the debate.

and Saunders adopt a pluralist line in their approach. Pluralists reject the Marxist association of ownership with control of mass media output, and claim that professional managers such as editors are primarily responsible for the output of the media. This essay will explore these two perspectives in more detail.

At this point I start the debate by giving the pluralist position and the managerial revolution thesis, but I also put in an evaluation in the last sentence.

The pluralist perspective can be seen in the work of Berle and Means, who have argued that now shareholding has become more widespread the control of firms no longer lies with individual owners. As a result of this fragmentation through shareholding, control of modern companies has passed to professional managers. This approach is known as the managerial revolution thesis and can be applied to the mass media. As far as Berle and Means are concerned, only professional managers have the necessary expertise to run large-scale companies, and as a result it is these managers who have control. According to managerialists, the content of the mass media is determined not by owners, but by managers. Conversely, Marxists would argue that editors and managers are merely another form of worker who can be dismissed or forced to resign if they do not follow the unwritten guidelines of the owners.

In this paragraph I continue the pluralist argument and illustrate it with a major item of recent news. You will need to find current examples.

Liberal pluralists, such as Whale, also dismiss the Marxist view that the mass media are controlled by their owners. They tend to dismiss the idea that media output is a reflection of the personal view of the owner or the manager. Rather, liberal pluralists argue that the content of the mass media is largely determined by audience demand. Following the death of Diana, Princess of Wales, public sentiment has meant that the mass media have now agreed to give the royal family a degree of privacy. According to a *Guardian*/ICM opinion poll, 81% of the public believe that the royal family's privacy should be protected by law. This is ironic given that the circulation of newspapers has gone up in the past whenever there has been a royal exclusive splashed across the front pages. Before Diana's death this was what the readership wanted. Consequently, the press paid the paparazzi vast sums for exclusive pictures, in order to win ratings battles with other newspapers. This example supports the notion that the audience plays a large part in determining media output.

It is, therefore, true to say that the content of the mass media is controlled by market forces. The media strive to please their audiences because if a mass media product does not have sufficient buyers, then the company which produces the product is likely to go out of business. This liberal pluralist argument is at least partially correct. Newspapers such as the *Today* newspaper have been forced to close. There are also a number of other factors which can influence the output of the mass media. The government has the power to prevent material being published through legislation like the Official Secrets Act. However, it can be argued that the government is losing its control over broadcasting, because satellite channels and the Internet can circumvent legislation.

Advertisers can also exert control over the output of the mass media. Women's glossy magazines, amongst others, are largely dependent on advertising revenue for their long-term survival, so they cannot afford to offend the companies which advertise with them. An example of the power of advertisers was demonstrated when the *Sun* ran one of its many xenophobic campaigns over the actions of French farmers. It printed a cut-out badge 'HOP OFF YOU FROGS'. The Citroen-Peugeot-Talbot group threatened to withdraw its advertising and the *Sun* quickly ended its campaign. These last two examples – government and advertiser intervention – illustrate the power of the state and commercial interests to dictate the output of the mass media, and suggest that managers are not necessarily primarily responsible for this output.

> This paragraph contains an important sentence from which you can learn an evaluation technique: 'This liberal pluralist argument is at least partially correct...'. The point here is that evaluation is not just about ripping an argument apart, it is about finding the good and bad in an argument. Students often lose sight of this.

Marxists would argue that ownership of the mass media is still concentrated in relatively few hands and that the argument that shareholding is widespread is inaccurate. Furthermore, Marxists claim that as economic power overrides all other types of power, in the long run ownership will dictate the output of the mass media. The 1997 British general election demonstrated that, as Marxists claim, managers are not primarily responsible. Prior to the general election, the Scottish edition of the *Sun* newspaper was running a pro-Scottish Nationalist, anti-Labour party campaign. It was forced to change its line to pro-Labour. Similarly, the London edition of the *Sun* was compelled to shift its political allegiance from the Conservative party to the Labour party, despite resistance from *Sun* managers such as its leader-writer and its deputy editor. According to the *Observer* newspaper, the *Sun*'s switch was due to orders from Ruport Murdoch in the United States. This interference by the owner culminated in the *Sun*'s headline, 'the *Sun* backs Blair'. Marxists are not arguing that the owners of the mass media necessarily direct the day-to-day operations and output of media corporations (although this is possible using satellite technology and the Internet). Instead, they argue that the employees of those companies, whether they are managers or in more mundane jobs, follow the unwritten dictates of their capitalist masters. Failure to do so could result in their dismissal.

> This section gives the Marxist position – economic power equals political power.

My conclusion concedes a number of influences over media output, but still makes sure that it evaluates by suggesting that the influence of ownership is most important.

In conclusion, this essay has demonstrated that there are a number of influences over media output. However, ultimately, it appears that the owners of the mass media have the final say on media content, in that they can demand that managers change stories if they contradict their unwritten dictates.

General comments

I hope by now that you understand the managerial revolution thesis and can see how straightforward this essay really is. Knowledge of this topic will also help you with the sociology of culture. Some of it fits in with the neo-Marxist Frankfurt School which claimed that the capitalist class could manipulate the media. However, do not fall into the trap of believing that society is made up of individuals who are puppets of the media.

Related questions

1   Examine the relationship between the ownership, control, and output of the mass media.

2   'Although it appears that managers run the mass media, in the long run owners have the final say.' How convincing do you find this argument?

3   How far is it true to say that the widespread nature of share ownership means that managers alone determine the content of the mass media?

To what extent does urbanisation automatically
lead to the loss of community?

In this answer it is probably best to refer to one of the older analyses of community, either
Tönnies's or Durkheim's would suffice. For this essay I chose to use the work of Tönnies
because a number of more up-to-date writings on community are based on his work. Before
attempting this essay, you should also be aware that the image of a golden age of community
is based on a myth. Your essay should reflect this, and aim to show that you cannot miss
what has never really existed.

Answer

Guidance notes

There are a number of definitions of 'community' and because of
this, any essay dealing with community will have problems. One
definition is that community is 'a geographical area'. A second
definition is that community is 'a local social system', that is, a
set of relationships within a specific area. A final definition of
community is 'a sense of shared identity'. Urbanisation refers to
the movement of the population from rural areas to towns and
cities. This kind of change has happened in Western societies for
over 200 years, and more recently, the process of urbanisation has
been occurring in poorer societies.

In this paragraph I have told the
reader that the definition of
community is problematic. I then
go on to give three separate
definitions. By doing this the
essay demonstrates knowledge
and understanding from the
outset.

Early writers, such as Tönnies, were concerned to explain the
change in social life from a rural to an urban way of life. Tönnies
used the term *Gemeinschaft* to describe the type of relationships
involved in rural living. By *Gemeinschaft*, Tönnies meant that the
social relationships in rural areas were close and intimate. The
word *Gemeinschaft* means that individuals relate to one another
in terms of friendship. In contrast, Tönnies used the term
Gesellschaft to describe the social relationships which were characteristic of urban living. *Gesellschaft* means association, and means
that individuals relate to one another in a rather impersonal
manner, as in the case of a visit to the supermarket where the

Some students are frightened by
German words which sometimes
appear in A-level textbooks. As
long as you can use the right
word in the right sociological
context, don't be afraid to include
them in your essay.

shopper puts the goods on the conveyor belt, the goods are scanned and priced, and then the till operator states how much the total is. In contrast, someone living in a small village may shop at the local shop where everybody knows each other and the relationship between the shopper and the shopkeeper is more personal. This early work of Tönnies suggests that urbanisation has led to a loss of community in the sense that a set of relationships within a specific area have disappeared. Nevertheless, Tönnies was aware that *Gemeinschaft* could also be found alongside *Gesellschaft* in urban areas.

> For this section of the essay I have applied the work of Willmott and Young. This should show you just how versatile some studies can be.

Later work which examined the notion of community in urban areas was put forward in Willmott and Young's study *Family and Kinship in East London*. This study looked at working-class life in Bethnal Green. It was expected that postwar Britain would see the breakdown of these types of communities, but Willmott and Young found that the community had characteristics of Tönnies's *Gemeinschaft*, in that the inhabitants of Bethnal Green had close-knit and personal relationships. In other words, despite being an urban area, Bethnal Green was not a community full of strangers demonstrating aspects of *Gesellschaft*. Their research shows that urbanisation does not automatically lead to the loss of community. Many individuals in contemporary Britain hark back to this golden age of community when 'everybody left their door open' and 'everyone knew each other'. It may be the case that this golden age of community never really existed. Even some government initiatives tend to discourage community spirit, for example, John Major's government introduced what can be described as a government-sponsored 'stitch-up thy neighbour' campaign whereby members of the public were encouraged to telephone a social security hotline and report neighbours suspected of making fraudulent claims. Paradoxically, some of these individuals are bound to be the same ones who hark back to the good old days. Tony Blair's Labour government has yet to do away with this hotline.

Feminists would be critical of the notion of a close-knit community by pointing to the differences in gender-based relationships. The women in the Bethnal Green study had close relationships with other women to whom they were related and the men close leisure relationships with other men, often involving pub life.

Willmott and Young's study also looked at Greenleigh, a new council estate to which some young married couples from Bethnal Green had moved. They found that life on the estate lacked the intimacy and closeness of Bethnal Green. The families at Greenleigh were home-centred and privatised, that is, they kept themselves to themselves. It can be argued that this is typical *Gesellschaft*. More evidence for this loss of community is found in Goldthorpe and Lockwood's research on the 'affluent worker'. Goldthorpe and Lockwood examined the life styles of Vauxhall car workers in Luton. This study revealed a distinct lack of community, and showed that the workers had opted for a family-centred lifestyle which was characterised by a largely privatised existence.

The work of Goldthorpe and Lockwood is also extremely versatile. In this instance, it has been used to show support for *Gesellschaft*.

However, Goldthorpe and Lockwood's work can be criticised. The major problem with their study is that the sample they used was not representative. The Vauxhall workers were mainly migrants who had moved to Luton to take relatively higher-paid car-assembly work. In addition, the majority of the sample fell into the 21–46 year age group. These factors mean that a sense of community would not have had time to develop. The same thing might be said about Willmott and Young's Greenleigh residents. A sense of community may have developed in the future but all of the residents were migrants and may have needed some time to settle into their new area.

About halfway through the essay, the response to the question changes direction. Note the language which is used to change direction.

Devine reviewed the 'affluent worker' study and discovered that some kind of community had indeed developed over time. She found that the original migrants to Luton were followed by their relatives, friends and neighbours from their previous existence. This enabled a traditional working-class community to be re-established. Again this would suggest that urbanisation does not automatically lead to a loss of community.

No matter what definition of community is used, the evidence which has been presented does not seem to indicate that urbanisation inevitably leads to a loss of community. If anything, it merely shows that the social relationships within communities have changed due to industrialisation, and that these social relationships are not in themselves as fixed as they were, but are subject to change with time. Marxists such as Castells point to the importance of economic change in understanding changes in community. The miners' strike in the mid-1980s demonstrated how whole communities came together to offer support for the miners and their families. However, it can also be argued that these same communities have been destroyed by the shut-down of mines. Nevertheless, evidence shows that there is quite a lot of community spirit in some inner-city areas in Britain today. Some inner-city areas have seen the development of Credit Unions which are run for and by local residents. It can be argued that in such instances such there is more sense of community than in middle-class suburbia. Some would claim that new developments in former run-down inner-city areas are attempting to recreate

This paragraph introduces a Marxist analysis of community and uses examples from 'real life'.

Once again, I have used a local example.

the old working-class neighbourhoods with their traditional community spirit. An example of this is Eldon village in inner-city Liverpool which is attempting to become a desirable and sought-after area. Another example is the gay area in Manchester known as the village, which prides itself on its community. The cafés, bars and restaurants are run by gays for gays. Urbanisation does not automatically lead to a loss of community.

Finally, the validity of research into the 'golden age of community' needs to be questioned, particularly research which is based on people's memories. It is important to be aware that the inhabitants of communities under investigation may be highly selective in their memories of traditional communities.

General comments

The sociology of community is a neglected area of study by schools and colleges offering A-level sociology. However, it is useful because it overlaps with the sociology of culture.

Related questions

1 'Community loss is just another urban myth.' Explain and discuss.

2 How far is it true to say that today's village is just as likely to be found in an urban area as a rural area?

3 To what extent are inner-city areas more likely to be characterised by crime than rural areas?

'The evidence of recent general elections shows
that class is no longer important in voting
behaviour.' Discuss.

Tackling the question

The election of a Labour government in May 1997 should allow strong candidates to show
off their knowledge of the most recent developments on research into voting behaviour.
Use *Politics Review* and *Sociology Review* to get the latest information. You could also use
the Internet if you have access to it. Weak candidates will rely on old research which tends
to explain Conservative successes since 1979. My answer has included whatever research
was available at the time of writing. Note that the question requires evidence of recent
general elections and not just the last one. Make sure you read the question properly or you
could come unstuck.

Answer

Guidance notes

Investigations into voting behaviour have traditionally looked at
the relationship between social class and voting. In the 1950s and
1960s, it was widely held that the working class voted Labour and
the middle class voted Conservative. According to Pulzer, 'class
is the basis of party politics, all else is embellishment and detail'.
However, election results increasingly indicate that individuals are
no longer voting along class lines. The Conservative party won four
consecutive general elections between 1979 and 1997 and it could
not have done so without a large percentage of the working-class
vote. It has been proposed, therefore, that social class is declining
as the major causal factor of voting behaviour. Until the election
of 1 May 1997 the Labour party seemed to be suffering as a result
of class dealignment, as it appeared to be losing its working-class
base. However, the Labour landslide victory in 1997 saw a reversal
of this trend. On this occasion, not only did the Labour party win
votes from the working-class section of society, but it also got
backing from many members of the middle class. It is doubtful
whether members of the working class who usually vote Conservative suddenly developed a working-class consciousness, just

The introductory paragraph sets
the voting behaviour discussion
into its post-Second World War
historical background. Do not
go back beyond this. Some
candidates have been known to
refer back to the work of Walter
Bagehot who was writing in the
nineteenth century. Even
references from 1945 to 1979
should be summed up in a
nutshell. The essay title specifies
recent elections, therefore this
answer refers to elections since
1979.

as it is doubtful whether members of the middle class who voted Labour can be seen to have taken this action through a process of proletarianisation. The fact that individuals who have voted Conservative for the last four elections switched votes to the Labour party demonstrates that voting behaviour is not determined by social class. This essay will examine the social class and voting behaviour debate in more detail.

The link between social class and voting behaviour was commented on by Butler and Stokes in the late 1960s. They argued that individuals were socialised into political party preferences. However, they also found evidence of class dealignment. As early as the 1950s around a quarter of the Conservative vote came from the working class, so evidence which questioned the importance of social class was already emerging. Nevertheless, the trend towards class dealignment has significantly increased over the last 18 years.

One explanation for the working-class Conservative vote is the embourgeoisement thesis. This suggests that there has been a growth in the affluence of many members of the working class, which has resulted in their developing middle-class attitudes and life styles, and consequently led them to vote Conservative. However, Goldthorpe and Lockwood's research on the affluent worker rejects this claim. They found that affluent manual workers still tend to vote Labour. Following the results of the 1997 general election, sociologists need to explore the reasons why so many members of the middle class voted Labour.

Crewe is an important figure in psephology (the study of voting behaviour) and is an essential part in any answer on recent voting trends. An answer which ignores Crewe won't get the highest marks.

The trend towards class dealignment has grown, especially in the last decade or so. According to Crewe, between 1945 and 1983 the Conservative share of the middle-class vote fell from 63% to 55%, whilst the Labour share of the working-class vote fell from 62% to 42%. Overall, class voting fell from 62% to 47%. On the basis of this evidence, commentators including Crewe argued that class voting has declined and that the lack of working-class solidarity is linked to a general loosening of the class structure. Over the last 15 years or so there has been a decline in manufacturing industry, and hence a decline in manual work. Simultaneously, there has been a rise in the service sector and in white-collar work. Crewe argued that as a result of these changes there were now two sections within the working class. He called these the traditional working class and the new working class. He defined the old working class as tending to live in the north of England in council house accommodation, to work in the public sector, and to be members of trade unions. By contrast, the new working class tend to live in the south of England, to be home buyers, to work in the private sector and be to non-unionised. Crewe claimed that the traditional working class was still likely to vote Labour whilst the new working class was more likely to vote Conservative. Crewe's explanation can be applied to the success of the Conservatives between 1979 and 1992. However, Crewe also argued that as a result of the fragmentation of the working class it was doubtful whether Britain would ever see another Labour victory. The success of Labour in May 1997 can be used to question Crewe's wider arguments. However, it is highly unlikely that any political commentator would suggest that the new working class have suddenly rediscovered their traditional working-class roots and as a consequence voted Labour. It can be argued that the working class are still as divided now as they were in the 1980s. Hence, some would suggest that there must be other factors apart from social class which influence voting behaviour.

However, Heath, Jowell and Curtice question the whole notion of class dealignment. They argue that rather than there being a decline in working-class support for the Labour party, the working class still tends to vote Labour, but there has been an actual decline in the size of the working class. Thus, Heath, Jowell and Curtice claimed that social class is still an important factor in voting behaviour, and that if the Labour party adopted the right policies to reflect this change in the class structure, then it was still possible for them to win a general election. The 1997 Labour victory obviously supports their argument, and was apparently based on a change in policies reflecting the change in the class structure.

According to Denver, who offered an explanation of the previous Conservative success, Britain had not only undergone a process of class dealignment, but also a period of party dealignment. This meant that there was a decrease in the number of people who possessed a persistent party identification. Denver claimed that the electorate was volatile because it was now politically educated, and this may have led it to question its traditional party ties. He also claimed that by 1983 traditional Labour voters had become dissatisfied with the Labour party's policies on defence. This may have led them to become detached from Labour and as a consequence to vote for a party other than Labour. In his analysis of Labour's victory in the 1997 general election, Denver claims that the evidence suggests that the electorate have become more volatile. He argues that the 1997 data shows that in comparison to voting behaviour in 1992 'there were massive defections from the Conservatives'. Using a BBC/NOP exit poll, Denver shows that nearly 30% of those who voted Conservative in 1992 switched their votes, mostly to Labour. Furthermore, Denver shows that the landslide victory was not caused by Conservative voters staying

In this section, I introduce Denver's early work on voting behaviour and link it to his latest research on the 1997 general election.

at home, because although the turnout was the lowest since the Second World War, the largest section of non-voters was found in Labour strongholds, that is poor, inner-city areas.

This paragraph also contains evidence from the 1997 general election, this time from Kavanagh. Note how it is linked to the earlier work of Heath *et al.*

Kavanagh's interpretation of the 1997 election results also shows evidence that class is no longer important in voting behaviour. Using a comparison of exit polls from 1992 and 1997, Kavanagh states that Labour made gains from all social classes, but that 'among C1s, or the lower middle-class, there was a massive swing to Labour'. This gives support to the ideas of Heath, Jowell and Curtice, that if the Labour party adopted policies which reflected changes in the class structure, they could still secure electoral victory.

At present the post-mortem on the 1997 general election continues. So far evidence has been produced which finds support for the notion of electoral volatility and class dealignment. However, other reasons will undoubtedly be advanced.

General comments

This type of essay always needs the latest research. Without it you will have difficulty in getting into the higher mark bands. You must also pay careful attention to the wording of the question. If the question only specifies 'elections', then you can write about local elections and European elections, which do not always follow the same patterns as general elections. You will then be able to make useful comparisons between the results of these different elections.

Related questions

1   To what extent is an individual's vote the result of a multiplicity of factors?

2   'Partisan dealignment has been a key element in general elections since 1979.' How far do you agree with this statement?

3   'In contemporary Britain, voters are likely to make a rational decision before casting their vote.' How far does the sociological evidence support this statement?

Evaluate the pluralist claim that power is distributed
among competing interest groups in society.

Tackling the question

This is a question which comes up in a variety of forms, so it is well worth revising. At its simplest level it asks you who has power in society. There are a number of theoretical positions which can be applied to this type of question. In this case I have used pluralism because that is what the question dictates. To give balance, I have used Marxism, but I could just as well have used classical élite theory, modern élite theory, neo-Marxist theory, and/or the work of John Scott. It is entirely up to the individual what theories he or she uses. In this case there is no right or wrong answer.

Answer

Guidance notes

According to Weber, power is the ability of individuals or groups to get their own way, even if this action is resisted by others. Pluralists accept Weber's view of power and use it in their attempt to measure who has power in society. For pluralists, those who have the most power will obviously be those who are able to get their own way most frequently. Hence, pluralists look at local and national government decision making to see if any group or groups consistently get their own way.

It is essential to define the term 'power' for this essay. In this instance I have used Weber because pluralists accept this definition, and therefore the essay needs it. In some cases, essays on power may require further exploration of the term. In that case I would advise you to look at Lukes' 'three faces of power'.

Classical pluralists believe that society is divided into a number of interest groups. Individuals in society may belong to one or more of these interest groups; for example, a teacher may belong to a trade union and Greenpeace. As a union member the teacher may be concerned with protecting his or her standard of living, and good provision of education in British schools; as a member of Greenpeace the same teacher may also be interested in environmental issues throughout the world. Individuals will belong to different interest groups according to their interests and beliefs. Classical pluralists would argue that each interest group will attempt to pressurise the government on behalf of its members.

Note that in this section, I use the term 'classical pluralist' rather than 'pluralist'. This is because later in the essay I will refer to a different but related form of pluralism, 'élite pluralism'. Weaker answers will simply refer to pluralism.

Here I present evidence to support classical pluralism from British and American studies. Note that if the question specified British society, the examiner would ignore any American material and therefore writing it would be a waste of time.

Note that this paragraph starts with 'one evaluation'. This signposts to the examiner the skill of evaluation in your answer. It is a good technique to use. This type of evaluation is called an 'internal critique'. All it means is that a sociologist from the same perspective is making the criticism rather than a sociologist from another perspective, which would be called an 'external critique'.

In this paragraph I give a general Marxist analysis of power, with references to events in modern Britain.

The government will mediate between different interest groups, and sometimes one interest group will gain a favourable outcome, sometimes another will be successful. Classical pluralists claim that no one interest group consistently gets its own way – they believe that power is distributed among competing interest groups in society.

There are a number of studies which support the classical pluralist perspective. Hewitt studied 24 British policy issues in the period 1944 to 1964 and concluded that no one group consistently got its own way. The classical pluralist perspective is also supported by the work of Grant and Marsh on the Confederation of British Industry (the CBI) which represents many of the top companies in Britain. They concluded that the CBI had little influence over government policy. Two studies of the American political system also support the classical pluralist argument. Pahl looked at local politics in New Haven, Connecticut and found no evidence of a dominant political group, while at a national level in American politics, Rose found evidence to support the pluralist contention that there are many groups which influence outcomes in politics.

One evaluation which has been made of the classical pluralist argument is that some groups are in a better position than others to influence government policy. Elite pluralists, such as Richardson and Jordan, accept that this is the case. They distinguish between 'insider' and 'outsider' pressure groups and claim that insider groups are recognised and consulted by the government, whereas outsider groups are less acceptable and are not consulted. Thus insider groups such as the National Farmers Union can influence policy on the Bovine Spongiform Encepalopathy (BSE) crisis because they will be consulted. However, outsider groups such as Greenpeace are less likely to be consulted on environmental issues such as the Newbury by-pass. Despite this problem with pluralism, pluralists still see Western societies as basically democratic.

A Marxist analysis of power can be used to evaluate the pluralist claim that power is distributed among competing interest groups in society. According to Marx, a group which is economically powerful is also politically powerful. In the case of modern industrial society, the bourgeoisie or capitalist class own the means of production and, for Marxists, it is this factor which gives them political power. According to Marxists, the state actually operates on behalf of the bourgeoisie. In Marx's own words, the government 'are the managing committee for the affairs of the whole bourgeoisie'. Marxists would claim that the bourgeoisie rule indirectly, and that the state makes decisions which tend to favour the bourgeoisie. Thus governments offer financial incentives to corporations to bring their factories to Britain, for example, Nissan and BMW (who bought out the British car company Rover). Furthermore, companies such as Sony have threatened to relocate their factories if the British government does not join the single European currency. This would mean the loss of many jobs and gives such companies considerable power. It is therefore difficult to see how power is equally distributed among competing interest groups, as most do not have the ability to hold the state to ransom. It is significant that New Labour now portrays itself at 'the party of business'. This in itself may not prove the Marxist argument but it does tend to lend support to it.

Miliband, a Marxist, uses an instrumental analysis of the British political system, that is, he sees the state as a tool or instrument of the bourgeoisie. Miliband tries to show that the British state is run by individuals from bourgeois backgrounds, and that the state is run on behalf of the bourgeoisie. Miliband was able to show that many of those occupying important state positions are from upper-class backgrounds. However, it is impossible to demonstrate clearly that the state rules on behalf of the bourgeoisie.

> Here I am using a variation of Marxism called an instrumentalist view.

Another Marxist, Poulantzas, rejects Miliband's arguments by offering a structuralist view of power. Poulantzas emphasises that the bourgeoisie is not a united group and that its members are often in direct competition with each other. Poulantzas claims that there is a governing class (the state) and a ruling class (the bourgeoisie). The separation of the governing class and the ruling class enables the governing class to operate on behalf of the whole bourgeoisie, and also provides the illusion of democracy. Although Miliband and Poulantzas differ in their analyses, they agree that power is not distributed among competing interest groups in society. Moreover, for Poulantzas, the only competition is between one bourgeois group and other bourgeois groups. Compared to the bourgeoisie, groups representing the interests of other individuals barely get a look in.

> At this point I use another variation of Marxism, a structuralist view. It acts as an internal critique of the instrumentalist view and as such scores evaluation marks.

Westergaard and Resler's assertion that power is only visible through its consequences seems to be appropriate in ascertaining whether or not power is distributed among competing interest groups. There is considerable evidence that those with most wealth have the most power. Thus the Thatcher government reduced the top band of income tax from 60% to 40% and

> In the conclusion I use a number of contemporary examples to conclude that the Marxist position is stronger than the pluralist position. If you wish to support the pluralist position, you

will have to find evidence to back up your arguments.

increased VAT. Similarly, during the period 1979 to 1991 the income of the top 20% of earners increased by around 20%, while the income of the bottom 20% fell by over 10%. In addition, Townsend has argued that since 1979, the poverty rate in Britain has increased dramatically, and has estimated that over 20% of the British population live in relative poverty. In comparison, Lord Iveagh receives one million pounds per year from the European Union for not farming part of his 23,000 acre Suffolk estate. The pluralist claim that power is distributed among competing interest groups in society can therefore be rejected.

General Comments

This essay can appear in a number of different forms. Sometimes the question will specify pluralism, as in this case. Sometimes it will specify other theories of power. Make sure you can distinguish between the different perspectives. Occasionally students confuse élite pluralism and élite theory (both classical and modern). If you know the material you will not make this mistake.

Related questions

1   Compare and contrast Marxist and élite theories of power.

2   'In modern society, there is no one group which consistently dominates decision making.' To what extent does the sociological evidence support this argument?

3   Evaluate the statement that 'in Britain today there is no ruling class'.

Question 34

'Religion no longer has power over the individual or society.' Evaluate the sociological evidence for this view.

Tackling the question

There are two parts to this question. Firstly, does religion have power over the individual? Secondly, does religion have power over society? This question is a variation of the secularisation debate. A good answer should be within the grasp of any well-prepared student. Your answer should consider the claims that secularisation affects both the individual and society and then evaluate the counter-eveidence. You may even find evidence to suggest that secularisation is occurring in one area and not the other. At the end you must come to a conclusion, is secularisation occurring for the individual, yes or no? Is secularisation occurring for society, yes or no?

Answer

The assertion that religion no longer has power over the individual or society is part of the argument that suggests that secularisation is occurring. According to Wilson, secularisation is the process whereby religious thinking, practices, and organisations lose social significance. This essay will evaluate the evidence for and against this argument.

Wilson presents a range of sociological evidence to support his argument that secularisation is occurring and, as a consequence, religion has less power over the individual and society. There is a considerable amount of statistical data which show that attendances and membership of the major British Christian religions are declining – for example, *Social Trends* shows that membership of the Church of England has declined by almost a million since 1970. In addition, baptisms, confirmations, and church weddings have also declined. Recently, representatives of the Church of England and the Methodists have held talks about a possible merger of the two churches. This can also be seen as an indication of secularisation.

Guidance notes

The introduction simply states that this is the secularisation debate and offers Wilson's definition of secularisation.

This second paragraph gives some statistical evidence to support Wilson. Do not get bogged down giving exact attendances or memberships – it will waste your time and you will not gain any more marks for it. The examiners do not expect you to remember precise numbers.

This is mainly an interactionist view of what the statistical data on religious activity mean; as such it is an evaluation.

However, as is often the case with statistical data, it is open to interpretation. Just because individuals no longer attend church does not necessarily mean that religion no longer has power over them. There are many reasons why individuals do not go to church, for example, many people now work on a Sunday, the traditional day of worship. Church attendance goes up dramatically at Christmas and Easter. This could be used as evidence to suggest that religion is still important to the individual. Just as church non-attendance is not necessarily indicative of atheism, so participation in religious services does not indicate an individual's religious belief. Demerath suggests that in some instances individuals – politicians, for example – may feel obliged to attend church in order to sustain a particular public image. Martin argues that the high church attendance of the past may have been due to the fear of an individual being labelled as deviant.

This paragraph is another evaluation of the statistical evidence but instead of interpreting the data, it presents different statistics which contradict the original statistics. Note how the last sentence links to the question.

Another problem with the statistical data is that it presents an incomplete picture of individual participation in religious activities. The data does not contain evidence on new religious movements such as the Mormons, which show an increase in membership. *Social Trends* shows that the Mormon church in the United Kingdom has doubled its membership since 1970. The same source indicates that some other non-Christian world religions, such as Sikhism, have quadrupled their membership in recent years, and in the case of Islam, membership has increased sixfold. This would suggest that, contrary to the notion of secularisation, religion still seems to be influential for many individuals.

According to Thompson, who cites a European Community survey, 76% of people believe in God. As Bellah points out, religion is 'individual and private' rather than 'collectivised and public'. Therefore, the statistical evidence on church membership and attendance will not reveal the extent to which religion has power over the individual.

This section contains another aspect of Wilson's secularisation argument, rationality. It also contains a number of evaluations of our individual rationality. Note that so far the answer has only looked at the power of religion over the individual. Remember that this is only part of the question.

Following Weber's argument that society would become more rational, Wilson claims that rational or scientific beliefs have reduced the power of religious belief over individuals. For example, scientific theory and scientific evidence have offered alternative, and for some more plausible, explanations for the development of the earth and the human race. According to Wilson, science has replaced the bible. One criticism of this view suggests that the rationality of individuals is over-stated. Thompson asks if rationality guides people's choice of partner or political party. Popular culture reveals a continuing belief in, and a concern with, the supernatural – witness the continuing belief in horo-scopes and the popularity of television programmes such as *The X-Files*. Berger and Luckmann admit that because science cannot answer all the questions there is still a need for religious belief which provides individuals with 'a universe of meaning', that is, a way of understanding the world. 'Fate' or 'God's will' is used to explain unexpected deaths; even the Dunblane tragedy has been ex-plained as 'God's will' by some. Berger and Luckmann claim that the need for a universe of meaning may result in forms of religion such as Transcendental Meditation which are more individual.

Another part of Wilson's argument that secularisation is occur-ring is that religion and religious institutions have less power over society. Wilson claims that religious institutions have declined in political power, in wealth, and in control and in-fluence over the state. Until the end of the nineteenth century, religion influenced areas of society such as education, health and welfare. The major type of education available to the working class in the nineteenth century was provided by Sunday schools. Even as late as the 1970s religious orders of nuns provided nursing services in British hospitals. Some Catholic schools in Britain today still have members of the clergy as headteachers, but the state now provides most education and welfare. Ac-cording to Wilson, the media have replaced the church as a source of information and guidance. Agony aunts (for instance) dispense moral guidance to readers. Wilson claims that the church is reduced to providing traditional rituals at Christmas and Easter. One piece of evidence which can be used to evaluate Wilson's suggestion that religion has lost its power over society is that high-status church leaders continue to speak publicly against inequalities in society. Successive Archbishops of Canterbury have continued to oppose social injustices despite being told to stay out of politics by various politicians. Thomp-son's work on new religious movements also suggests that religion has played an active part in defining society's moral boundaries by their campaigns for family values and against sex and violence in the media. However, it can be argued that religious groups have been largely unsuccessful in their attempts. For example, religious leaders failed in their attempt to prevent Sunday opening for shops.

This section links to the part of the question which deals with religion's power over society. It is dealt with briefly then evaluated in the same paragraph.

In conclusion, it is not clear that religion has lost its power over the individual or society. Despite the increase in membership for new religious movements, participation in institutionalised Christianity has declined. However, Hay claims that 'well over a

Here I reject the claim that religion has lost its power over the individual or society on the basis of the evidence that I have produced. You might produce different evidence and a different conclusion.

third of all women and just under a third of all men in Great Britain claim to have experienced some sort of religious experience'. In addition, evidence shows that almost 70% of Britons believe in God. While the churches continue to produce reports on social issues in an attempt to influence government policy on employment, poverty and housing, it will not be safe to say that religion has no power over society.

General comments

Other questions on secularisation may require a wider range of evidence on this topic. For example, you may need to refer to the United States with its drive-in churches and tele-evangelism. You are likely to find articles on this in periodicals such as *Sociology Review*. Other evidence that you could refer to on questions on secularisation includes the proliferation of new religious movements.

Related questions

1   Discuss the claim that the secularisation thesis offers the best account of religious beliefs and practices in Britain today.

2   'The growth of new religious movements has signalled the end of religion.' How far does the evidence support this view?

3   How far is it true to say that Britain has undergone a process of secularisation?

Question 35

'The role of religion is to justify and maintain inequalities in society.' How far is this true of religion in modern society?

Tackling the question

This question is a partial version of the classic debate between Marx and Weber on the role of religion. Many students will be familiar with this debate to a greater or lesser extent. Some students will even be able to embellish it by referring to the functionalist contribution. The key to success in this essay is to link it constantly to the question. There are at least eight instances in this answer of a 'tie' to the question.

Answer

Guidance notes

The statement that the role of religion is to justify and maintain inequalities in society is most closely associated with Marxist sociology. This essay will examine the Marxist perspective on religion and will use the functionalist perspective and the Weberian perspective to evaluate it.

According to Marx, alienation is the natural result of the social conditions and relationships in class societies such as capitalism. Alienation means that individuals remain unfulfilled in all areas of their life – at home, at work and at leisure. Marx argued that individuals' religious beliefs reflect their alienation, and claimed that religion becomes a substitute for everything that is missing in an individual's life. It is possible that the hippy movement of the 1960s was a result of the alienation of young people. It is worth noting that some political songwriters of the 1960s, such as Bob Dylan, have now turned to religion. It may be that this conversion is a result of the hippy movement failing to achieve utopia on earth. However, songwriters like Dylan may have turned to religion in the hope of finding utopia in the afterlife. Evidence suggests that new religious movements tend to recruit alienated young people who are looking for answers to the world's problems. New religious movements can be seen as a modern-

A brief opening which locates the statement within a Marxist perspective and then maps out the essay. You should aim to do this in your introductions whenever possible.

A brief explanation of the Marxist position which continues into the next paragraph. I have mentioned Bob Dylan to explain why alienation can result in individuals turning to religion. Can you think of any modern-day artists who have turned to religion?

day replacement for the hippy movement. Some young people are able to find comfort in the beliefs of new religious movements in order to escape from their unsatisfactory lives in wider society.

Marx believed that religion prevents individuals from understanding their position within society. He argued that religion is an illusion which prevents the development of the individual. This can be explained by analysing one of Marx's most famous statements on religion, that it is 'the opium of the people'. This statement is frequently misunderstood to mean that the ruling class, that is the capitalist class, fed the subject class, that is the working class, with religion in order to keep them in their place. Marx wrote 'as in religion, man is governed by the products of his own brain'. Marx meant that the illusion of religion was created by the human race itself and that religion and gods do not exist outside the human imagination. For Marxists, religions originate in oppressed classes, as was the case with Christianity, which became popular among Roman slaves. The hope of finding a place in heaven would have made slavery more tolerable.

Marx argued that religion, as the 'opium of the people', takes away the pain of the masses and makes life bearable. Many religions offer some kind of wonderful life after death for the faithful who have led a good life, and it is possible that the promise of a better life after death helps to keep people in their place. Marxists believe that this can defuse working-class protest and prevent individuals from rebelling against inequalities caused by the capitalist system. It is important to note that this is not the result of a capitalist conspiracy, but rather the result of the social conditions produced by class societies. Furthermore, religions frequently make a virtue out of suffering: to Buddhists, for example, all life is suffering. Some individuals do not expect anything other than suffering when they are alive. An additional point is that many religions are waiting for the end of the world, when everything wrong on earth will be put right and justice will be served. Mormons, for example, are awaiting the second coming of Christ, when the wicked will be punished and the righteous will be saved. Some religious beliefs actively support existing unequal social arrangements, for example Hinduism and the caste system of stratification.

This section applies part of the secularisation thesis to the question and then proceeds to an evaluation based on contemporary evidence of religious beliefs in Britain.

Some sociologists, such as Wilson, argue that secularisation is occurring in Britain today. Secularisation means that religious ideas and institutions are losing their influence over society. If Wilson is correct, then it can be argued that the Marxist analysis of religion cannot be applied to Britain today because religion is no longer important in modern Britain and cannot therefore be seen as keeping people in their places. Wilson does not see religion as justifying or maintaining inequalities in society. Support for Wilson can be found in the most recent research on church-going in England – *UK Religious Trends* – which shows that only 10% of the population regularly attend church. However, as Davie points out, there is a large gap between church attendance and belief in God. According to Davie, despite poor church attendance, 70% of individuals still believe in God.

The Marxist contention that the role of religion is to justify and maintain inequalities is weakened by the fact that in Britain church leaders have actively campaigned against some of the in-equalities of capitalism. Some religious leaders saw the Thatcher-led Britain of the 1980s as based on greed, and spoke out against it. A *Daily Mail* survey of 1996 found that the Church of England synod (a form of council) felt that the most important moral issues of the day were unemployment, the environment, and the third world. These economic and social issues outweighed other issues which are more usually associated with the church, such as extra-marital sex, abortion and homosexuality. This is not a case of religion justifying and maintaining inequality. Furthermore, church-commissioned reports, such as 'Faith in the City' have openly criticised British government policy. For example, the report claimed that the Thatcher government's policies for the inner city were actually 'making the plight of some classes of citizens worse'.

> This is an evaluation of Marxism which uses material you could find in many A-level sociology textbooks.

Further afield, Christian institutions try to redress the balance between rich countries and poor countries. Organisations like Christian Aid organise overseas development aid for projects in the third world. In addition, in many Central and South American countries, a number of clergy from different faiths (for example, the Jesuits, a teaching order of the Roman Catholic church) teach a brand of liberation theology. Liberation theology is a religious teaching which tells the people that they have a God-given duty to free themselves from social injustice and inequality. For some liberation theologists, this fight can even include armed struggle. Thus the oppressed are being actively encouraged to overturn the inequalities in society rather than accept them, even if this means bloodshed.

Weber agreed with Marx that religion could maintain and justify inequalities in society, but claimed that this was not its only role. For Weber, religion had the potential to be a force for social change. He based his argument on his study of the rise of capitalism. He argued that there was an 'elective affinity', that is a close relation-ship, between Ascetic Protestantism, such as Calvinism, and the

> Another evaluation of Marxism, this time using the Weberian argument. Watch that you get the wording of this exactly right. Some textbooks, some teachers and even examiners have been known

to make mistakes over the term 'elective affinity'. I explain its meaning in the answer, and I also explain what it does not mean.

rise of capitalism. This does not mean that Ascetic Protestantism caused capitalism. However, according to Weber, Ascetic Protestantism contained within its beliefs elements which assisted the development of capitalism, for example, an attitude to wealth which held that profit should not be spent wastefully, but reinvested in business. This reinvestment is a prerequisite for capitalism. For Ascetic Protestants, success on earth was seen as a sign of salvation. In an address to the Church of Scotland, Thatcher claimed that it was 'our Christian duty to make money'.

The major problem with Weber's work is the 'chicken and egg' issue of which came first, Ascetic Protestantism or capitalism? It is possible to date Ascetic Protestantism, but impossible to date capitalism accurately. Marxists would argue that capitalism pre-dates Ascetic Protestantism and therefore Weber's work is based on a false premise.

Functionalists would also reject the Marxist argument that the role of religion is to justify and maintain inequalities in society. According to Parsons, religion helps to maintain social order in modern society. It does this by providing explanations of unforeseen events, such as unexpected death, and so helps people to deal with the uncertainties of life by making sense of such events. For example, fundamentalist Christians see suffering as a punishment for sins, as in the case of gays and AIDS. In this way religion promotes social stability.

I conclude on the Marxist side by claiming that capitalism is still capitalism despite religious interference. Obviously, your own essays can end with a different conclusion. But remember, whatever you say, you must support it with evidence.

In conclusion, some might claim that religion, far from maintaining inequalities in modern societies, can bring about social change, for example Desmond Tutu's role in helping to bring about majority rule in South Africa. However, Marxists would argue that change from a white-ruled capitalist society to a black-ruled capitalist society merely confirms their argument that religion maintains and justifies inequalities because nothing has changed: people are still being exploited and consequently alienated by capitalism. Furthermore, Marxists would claim that the church-based reports and outspoken bishops have not changed British society. In fact, the number of people who live in poverty in Britain has increased during the period of these church reports.

General comments

Some students who are strong believers in a religious faith have problems with essays concerning religion. This is especially the case with perspectives like Marxism which challenge their beliefs. If you are such a student, remember that sociology is not a matter of faith, you do not have to believe what you are taught, or what you write. You only have to present a coherent reasoned answer.

Related questions

1   'Religion maintains the status quo in society.' Explain and discuss.

2   To what extent is it true to say that religion is not necessarily a conservative force in society?

3   How far has functionalist theory contributed to our understanding of the role of religion?